D1217404

A PICTORIAL HISTORY OF WESTERNS

Front endpaper: *The Wild Bunch*
Back endpaper: *Shenandoah*
Opposite: Lee Marvin in *Cat Ballou*
Overleaf: Yul Brynner and Steve McQueen in
The Magnificent Seven

A PICTORIAL HISTORY OF WESTERNS

MICHAEL PARKINSON & CLYDE JEAVONS

Special Picture Research by John Kobal

GONDOLA

HAMLYN
London · New York · Sydney · Toronto

CONTENTS

First published 1972 by The Hamlyn Publishing Group Limited

First published 1983 as a Hamlyn Gondola Book by
The Hamlyn Publishing Group Limited
London · New York · Sydney · Toronto
Astronaut House, Feltham, Middlesex, England

© Copyright 1972 The Hamlyn Publishing Group Limited
© Copyright 1983 this revised edition

All rights reserved. No part of this publication may be
reproduced, stored in a retrieval system, or transmitted,
in any form or by any means, electronic, mechanical,
photocopying, recording or otherwise, without the permission
of The Hamlyn Publishing Group Limited.

ISBN 0 600 37307 X

Text set in 12/14 pt Century Schoolbook 227
Captions set in 11/13 pt Univers Medium 689

Printed in Hong Kong

INTRODUCTION

When I was a kid, some of my best friends were cowboys. I knew them all – Hopalong Cassidy, Gene Autry, Randolph Scott and Roy Rogers were intimate acquaintances. I shared their every adventure, winced when they were in danger, cheered when they triumphed. Being part of what is called 'The Cinema Generation', I went to the cinema four nights a week. We paid threepence to sit in the first four rows, which consisted of hard board seats designed by a firm specializing in torture chambers. The area we occupied was called by many names, none of which related to the official description of 'Front Stalls'. To us it was 'the spitting ring', the Manager called it his 'jungle', and to the posh patrons in the balcony it was a cross between an ashtray and a spittoon.

But it didn't matter. Those were the golden days of the cinema when we turned our backs on the grimness of post-war Britain and craned our necks and gazed upward, eyes bulging like chapel hat pegs at anything and everything Hollywood pushed our way. For me the cinema was many things. It was here I fell in love for the first time. Her name was Joan Leslie, and when she kissed Robert Hutton in *Hollywood Canteen*, I knew the first terrible pangs of unrequited love. It was in the cinema I suffered my first attack of hero worship. His name was Robert Mitchum and I spent a deal of my time as a teenager persuading my eyelids to droop like his did. I tried to walk like John Wayne, talk like Cary Grant, light a fag like Bogy. Indeed, it was Bogy who persuaded me to a career in journalism. I saw him in that trilby, phone nestled to his shoulder, saying, 'Hold the front page', and all thoughts of being an engine driver or a brain surgeon were swept from my mind.

I loved films (I still do), but most of all I liked Westerns (I still do). Any list of my ten favourite films would include at least three Westerns. In the days when I rode shotgun for Hopalong Cassidy, the Wild West seemed a simple place to be. There were goodies and there were baddies, and you could tell them apart because the goodies had all the nicest horses and the baddies struck matches on their backsides. It was this simple division between good and evil with good triumphing that was so beguiling.

My favourite cinema in those days was in a neighbouring village where the Manager had the good sense to replace the back row of the stalls with half a dozen saddles stuck on poles. Competition for those 'seats' was fierce, as can be imagined, but many's the time that I've fought my way to the front of the queue, jumped into the saddle and ridden through a ninety-minute horse opera. There aren't many people who can claim they first became saddle-sore in a cinema – but I did. That was a long time ago and a lot has changed since. The world has changed, and so has the Wild West. It's a different world nowadays, nearer reality perhaps than the fantasy West of my youth. But it's still beguiling, more now than ever before.

What follows is a fond look at the Western in all its forms, from the beginning to the present time. It is dedicated to anyone who got dust in his eyes from sitting too near the screen.

MICHAEL PARKINSON

9

The FILMS

In 1902, two members of a notorious and audacious gang of outlaws known as The Wild Bunch came to realize that civilization was fast closing in on the open ranges of the West and the time had come to find easier pickings elsewhere. Taking with them a pretty schoolteacher called Etta Place and $30,000 in stolen banknotes, they travelled East to New York for one last fling and then lit out for an unsuspecting South America.

The outlaws' names were Robert Leroy Parker and Harry Longbaugh – better known as Butch Cassidy and the Sundance Kid. They were virtually the last of the legendary badmen of the Western plains – and probably the most spectacular.

The following year, with a timing which in retrospect looks marvellously apt, Edwin S. Porter made the first recognizable Western film. It was called *The Great Train Robbery* and it became the blueprint for the countless films which, in the seventy-seven years of the cinema's history, have attempted to depict the exploits, real and imaginary, of the pioneers, frontiersmen, lawmen and bandits of the sprawling American West. It was the modest beginning of one unique mythology (the Western) building on another (the West itself), and the first visual evocation of a thrilling and epic folklore.

The Great Train Robbery was not, strictly speaking, the very first Western. A number of earlier vignettes had shown scenes of cattle round-ups

Left: James Stewart in *The Man from Laramie* (1955), with Alex Nicol, Mike Mazurki and Wallace Ford. *Top: The Professionals* (1966).

and buffalo herds – even Buffalo Bill himself – and had reconstructed Western incidents already popularized and over-glamorized by the dime novel, such as hold-ups and scalpings. In 1898, W.K.L. Dickson had directed for the Edison Company a tableau called *Cripple Creek Bar-room*, complete with cowboys, dudes, a suspiciously masculine-looking barmaid, and a large pitcher marked 'Red Eye', and this has a stronger claim to being the 'first' Western.

But *The Great Train Robbery* was undoubtedly the first creative film drama made in America and coincidentally it happened also to be a Western. Despite its naivety and its obviously Eastern locations, it was a remarkable film for its time, employing a primitive form of editing, techniques such as the superimposition of a moving exterior scene on the 'window' of an interior set, and, at the end of the film (or maybe at the beginning, since its function was never clearly understood and its position arbitrary) a dramatic close-up of the chief villain (George Barnes) pointing his six-gun at the audience. It also, in its ten-minute length, set the classical story-pattern for subsequent Westerns – crime, chase and retribution – and stamped out a number of familiar ingredients, such as the fight on top of the train and the final shoot-out.

Porter never recaptured in his later films the narrative flair which is apparent in *The Great Train Robbery*, although he directed more Westerns, including in 1907 *Rescued from an Eagle's Nest*, which is notable mainly for having D.W. Griffith in the leading role. But *The Great Train*

Robbery was a big commercial success as well as a cinematic milestone, and it inspired a rash of imitations sufficient to set the genre well and truly in motion. Train robberies were still a fact of life in the first decade of the century, so this theme retained its popularity; but other formulas began to develop also, most importantly a trend away from groups of goodies and baddies and towards individual heroes and villains. Another Edison film of 1906, *A Race for Millions*, went so far as to conclude with a gun-duel on main street (most of which was a very obvious painted set).

This trend was leading inevitably up to the one major ingredient which was so far lacking in the Western – the star-hero. Audiences needed a central character on which to concentrate their attention, and he suddenly transpired in 1908 in the stocky person of G.M.Anderson, soon to be known almost exclusively as Broncho Billy. Anderson's rise to stardom was almost accidental. He had talked his way into a small part in *The Great Train Robbery* and then set about learning the movie business as both actor and director. He formed with George K. Spoor what was to become one of the most distinguished of the early movie studios – Essanay – and made one significant move by setting up a West Coast studio in California, close to the authentic geography which was swiftly to become an obvious vital part of Western film-making. (Although as late as 1915 Edison were still using Eastern locations – as exposed most embarrassingly in *The Corporal's Daughter* which, in a scene showing the cavalry riding out of a fort, carelessly allows a modern main road, complete with drain, to slip into the frame.)

Anderson recognized the need for an identifiable cowboy hero, but he had had no intention at first of casting himself in the part – a step he was, however, forced to take when he could find no one else available for the lead in a short Western called *Broncho Billy and the Baby*.

The film was a remarkable success, audiences taking readily to the Broncho Billy character: the courageous, basically decent good-badman prepared to sacrifice his freedom to help a child in distress. They liked also (and, before the glamorizing star-system, were more ready to accept) the air of reality which Broncho Billy got from Anderson's rugged, plain, amiable, bulky and boyishly gauche appearance.

In seven years Billy appeared in something approaching five hundred one- and two-reelers, sticking to the noble, faintly tragic lone-rider characterization with which he began the series.

to 'B' Western standards compared with the William S. Hart and Tom Mix vehicles which began to supersede them – but their popularity was immense and they firmly established the Western's enduring and universal appeal as well as its penchant for prolific output.

The Western also profited in its formative years from the fact that two of the greatest film-makers of the cinema's early period cut their directorial teeth on the genre: David Wark Griffith and Thomas H. Ince. Before their arrival on the scene – and before Griffith in particular had begun to develop a language of film and to lay the foundations of cinema as an art form – the Western had little shape or style.

Certainly there was no *lack* of Westerns following the success of the first Broncho Billy productions – now-extinct companies such as Selig, Lubin, Bison and Vitagraph were churning them out for all they were worth; and already-familiar themes were getting the familiar Hollywood treatment. The last-minute cavalry rescue was becoming a cliché; Custer, Jesse James and Davy Crockett were being credited with their first apocryphal exploits; fictional characters such as O. Henry's 'Cisco Kid' were being elevated into the mythology of the historical West; and the Red Indian was already being presented with an ambivalence which showed him to be incorrigibly savage and bloodthirsty on the one hand and noble, romantic and unjustifiably persecuted on the other. But the industry's enthusiasm for the Western could not make up for its lack of consistency and direction and, Broncho Billy apart, the genre was beginning to look played out by 1910.

Griffith and Ince, however, provided the creative impetus that was so sorely needed. Griffith, of course, did not devote himself solely to Westerns, and his epic masterpieces have little to do with the genre as such, but horse operas nevertheless played an important part in his early career.

In them, he developed his innovations and practised his editing techniques, and they were an ideal outlet for his love and grasp of spectacle and excitement. He aimed at authenticity, filming most of his Westerns on the West Coast, and he preferred action, theme and character to detailed plot.

Fighting Blood, which he made in 1911, has lately become recognized as the classic film of Griffith's early career, and an extremely influential Western. It concerns a Civil War veteran and his family, pioneer settlers on the Dakota frontier, battling against a band of Sioux Indians. The son has ridden off for help, and finally the cavalry arrive to

Far left top: Thomas Ince's The Way of a Mother (1913). Far left centre: William S. Hart in The Tiger Man (1918), with Jane Novak; Lambert Hillyer directed. Far left bottom: Hart as Wild Bill Hickok (1923). Left: Ethel Grey Terry played Calamity Jane opposite Hart's Hickok. Above: The Gunfighter, directed by Hart himself in 1917. Below left: Tom Mix in The Broncho Twister (1927). Below: Mix with Dan Clark, the cameraman who shot most of his features, and Art Rosson, later a second-unit director for Cecil B. DeMille.

perform the rescue. A simple enough story, but one given style and suspense of remarkable maturity by Griffith's instinctive cinematic touches and striking compositions: children cowering under a bed; a long column of cavalry galloping across the screen in long-shot, the head of the column a few moments later entering the frame in close-up to suggest a vast number of riders between front and rear; and the climactic battle between cavalry and Indians filmed in panoramic long-shot from a hilltop to take in the whole scene. These were advanced techniques, however, for 1911, and it took *Birth of a Nation* four years later to establish them as acceptable innovations.

Griffith's other notable Westerns at this period were *The Last Drop of Water* (1911), a precursor of the 1923 epic *The Covered Wagon* (and arguably the more exciting), *The Battle at Elderbush Gulch* (1913), which has Lillian Gish and Mae Marsh as Eastern girls in conflict with some decidedly savage Indians, and *The Massacre*, an austere depiction of the Custer massacre which is both anti-war and sympathetic to the Indian point of view. After 1913, apart from an inflated feature of 1919 called *Scarlet Days*, Griffith and the Western parted company.

Ince was more a creative producer than a director and, compared to Griffith, his artistic contribution is small. But his influence on the Western and on those who worked under him was immense. He concentrated far more than Griffith on story and content, and he established new standards in efficient shooting methods, meticulous script preparation and authenticity. His staging and showmanship were particularly impressive, and he employed the resources of an entire Wild West Show, complete with real cowboys and Indians, to film such spectacles as *War on the Plains* (1911). In order to achieve respectability in his movies he also introduced strong moral elements, his wayward characters suffering severe retribution. His endings were often, in fact, excessively and unnecessarily tragic.

Ince's best Westerns were probably those with Indian themes, such films as *The Indian Massacre* (1912) and *The Heart of an Indian* (1913) showing remarkable objectivity and sympathy for the Indian as well as the white pioneer, and condemning the extermination of the tribes. Latterly in his career Ince's creativity dwindled and his innate vanity took over (he indulged a fondness for appearing frequently in the credits of films he

Far left: Tom Mix in a characteristic publicity pose, and (*below*) finding romance on an observation car in *The Texan* (1920), one of many Mix features directed by Lynn Reynolds. *Above and below:* Scenes from James Cruze's *The Covered Wagon* (1923), the first epic Western, with J. Warren Kerrigan, Lois Wilson and, helping to raise the flag, Ernest Torrence.

had anything – or sometimes very little – to do with), but in 1914 he made one great fortuitous contribution to the Western by giving a forty-four-year-old veteran stage actor the starring role in a feature film called *The Bargain*. The actor was William S. Hart.

Hart entered movies at a time when the Western had reached a low ebb. Tom Mix was on the scene, but as yet had made no impact; Griffith had moved on to greater things and Ince's best work was behind him; the major companies were in a rut of standard one- and two-reeler productions; and only Broncho Billy was maintaining the Western's popularity, but without making any further substantial contribution to the art of the genre.

Hart was exactly the right man to develop the Western's feature-length potential and to inject into it the seriousness, dedication and apparent realism which were to mark his films out as the first 'adult' Westerns. Superficially, Hart is remembered as the archetypal good-badman, the lone rider ready to be reformed by the love of a good woman (usually half his age); a gaunt, silent figure in a boy-scout hat crouched menacingly behind a pair of six-guns.

In fact, Hart was far more than a nostalgic screen presence. As actor, director and writer, in a film career which lasted little more than ten years, he became the first man to put poetry into the Western,

Far left top: Harry Carey and Irene Rich in John Ford's *Desperate Trails* (1921). *Above left:* Mary Pickford as she appeared in *A Romance of the Western Hills* (1910), one of D.W.Griffith's formative Westerns. *Left:* William K. Howard's *White Gold* (1927) with George Bancroft. *Top and above:* Dustin Farnum in Cecil B. DeMille's *The Squaw Man* (1913), a story which DeMille remade twice, in 1918 and 1931. The heavy brandishing the guns is Billy Elmer; the Indian girl about to turn the tables, Princess Red Wing.

and it is he more than any other who founded the best traditions of Western film-making.

Hart's films were in direct contrast to those of his only contemporary of comparable stature, Tom Mix, whose highly entertaining product owed more to the circus and rodeo than to the actual frontier. Hart's concern from the start was to put the truth of the West on film, and he maintained a remarkable standard in a prodigious output. Later, he began to over-emphasize the sentimental and chivalrous sides of his screen character to the detriment of the films' credibility and popularity, but up to 1919 his record was impressive.

Many of Hart's Westerns were outstanding by any standards – *The Narrow Trail* (1917), which contained some of his best riding shots; *The Aryan* (1916), Hart's own choice as his best film; *Blue Blazes Rawden* (1918); *Branding Broadway* (1918), a lighthearted 'Western' set in New York in which he lassoes the villain in Central Park, a modern urban theme which he had tried earlier in *Between Men* (1915); *The Toll Gate* (1920), moving, exciting and *un*sentimental; and *Wild Bill Hickok* (1923), a pleasingly accurate biography of the famous lawman, accurate that is save for Hart's self-confessed lack of a physical likeness. But the two Hart films which are regarded as his supreme masterpieces are the well-known and still-popular *Hell's Hinges* (1916), and *Tumbleweeds*, his last film, made in 1925.

C. Gardner Sullivan, Hart's favourite screen writer, provided the meaty story for *Hell's Hinges*, which among other marvellous ingredients contains some of the silent cinema's best and most evocative subtitles. A weak preacher (Jack Standing) is sent to satisfy the religious needs of Hell's Hinges, 'a good place to "ride wide of"' and 'a gun-fighting, man-killing, devil's den of iniquity'.

Troubleshooter Blaze Tracey (Hart) has been instructed by villain Silk Miller (Alfred Hollingsworth) to run the preacher out of town as soon as he arrives, but the sight of the preacher's sister Faith (Clara Williams) stops him short ('One who is evil, looking for the first time on that which is good') and eventually he becomes her protector, even succumbing to religious conversion ('I reckon God ain't wantin' me much, Ma'am, but when I look at you I feel I've been ridin' the wrong trail') although the preacher has meanwhile succumbed to the allures of the local vamp (Louise Glaum). Then the action starts: the saloon gang burn down the church and shoot the preacher; Tracey appears, enraged, and after killing Miller sets fire to the entire town ('Hell needs this town, and it's goin' back, and goin' damn quick!'). Finally, Tracey leads Faith away to the mountains ('Whatever the future, theirs to share together . . .').

Hell's Hinges is above all a beautifully made film, basically spectacular but full of characteristic individual touches (as he reads the Bible for the first time, Tracey smokes and keeps his whisky handy) and one of cameraman Joseph August's highest achievements.

Tumbleweeds was Hart's farewell to the screen, a great Western epic which made hardly any concessions to the easy-going, streamlined, stunt-packed Tom Mix features which were by now highly popular and whose production values Hart refused to imitate, preferring retirement. The highlight of *Tumbleweeds* was a splendid reconstruction of the Cherokee landrush, exciting, beautifully edited, eschewing glib stuntwork, containing some travelling shots of pure poetry, and through it all Hart giving one of his finest exhibitions of horse-riding at speed. Later reconstructions of this event – for example, in the two versions of *Cimarron* –

can claim to be bigger, but none has matched the vitality of Hart's.

Clever detail still abounded in this film, its epic qualities notwithstanding: for example, the scene where Hart exposes a 'sooner' (one who has illegally anticipated the landrush by staking his claim too soon) by testing the 'sweat' on the man's horse – the 'sweat' turns out to be soapsuds!

At the beginning of the film, Hart prophetically remarks to some companions as the cattle herds leave the Cherokee Strip: 'Boys, it's the last of the West.' For Hart, it was the last of the Western. In 1939 *Tumbleweeds* was reissued with the addition of music and effects and a poignant eight-minute prologue beautifully delivered by Hart on his own ranch. In it he bade farewell to his audience, and it provides a fitting obituary to the man who brought to the Western an artistry and respectability which no amount of 'B' Western gimmickry could erode.

By the time Hart's career had ended, Tom Mix had joined Fox, graduated to features, and become the leading Western star, one whose showmanship, polish and unashamedly escapist format was to exert a dominant influence on the Western for twenty-five years or more, engendering the long reign of the 'B' Western throughout the thirties and inspiring a succession of immaculately costumed Saturday matinée idols (and their mounts) from Ken Maynard, Hoot Gibson and Tim McCoy to Gene Autry and Roy Rogers (not to mention 'Champion', 'Trigger' and other four-legged friends).

Few of Mix's best Westerns have survived, owing to the ravages of fire and chemical decomposition, but of those that have, *Sky High* (1922) is regarded as a prime example. Fast-paced and full of action, it demonstrates Mix's ability and willingness to perform most of his own stunts, no matter how

From the left: Easy Going (1926) with Buddy Roosevelt, minor star from the twenties; J. Farrell MacDonald and Tom Santschi in Ford's *Three Bad Men* (1926); two scenes from *The Iron Horse* (1924), Ford's first classic Western, with MacDonald again on hand.

dangerous or bruising they proved to be – and with the location in this case being the Grand Canyon, they could be hazardous indeed.

Although action in the form of fist-fights, chases and stunts was the order of the day in Mix's films, violence and death were kept to a minimum, a tradition which was to be maintained throughout the 'B' Western era, along with low comedy, animal-appeal (*Just Tony*, made in 1922 as a tribute to his horse, is adjudged one of Mix's best films of the period) and the intrusion of modern elements, such as aircraft and motor-cars (later taken to ridiculous extremes in Rogers and Autry vehicles with flying wings, jet-rockets and atomic missiles).

Other superior Mix Westerns of the twenties, distinguished mainly for their brilliant stuntwork, were *The Lone Star Ranger*, a Zane Grey adaptation; *The Rainbow Trail*, made when Mix was at his peak; and *The Great K and A Train Robbery*, notable for a spectacular fight on top of a fast-moving freight train. Latterly, and particularly with the coming of sound, Mix's films suffered some deterioration, but the cream of his work remains the most successful series of horse operas ever made, if not the best, and he undoubtedly set a pattern for the Western and its stars which was to be maintained for more than a quarter of a century.

This is not to say that with the coming of Tom Mix a serious approach to the Western disappeared altogether. What was lacking was any kind of urge to produce large-scale Westerns, particularly as Hart was beginning to bow out. In 1923, however, the genre received the boost it needed with the making of the first genuine Western epic and one of the most important films in the history of the Western: James Cruze's *The Covered Wagon*. Its success was such that serious film-makers from Hart and John Ford onwards were stimulated into creating and maintaining an epic tradition in the Western – one which has occasionally lapsed but happily never died out.

In view of its importance, it is mildly surprising to find on viewing the film nearly fifty years later that it is really rather dull. The scenes are statically shot and what little action there is suffers from unimaginative editing and some obvious studio inserts. It is flawed, too, by a slack disregard for authenticity – most notoriously in having its wagonmaster invite open attack by Indians by camping his wagon train in a box canyon, as a scathing William S. Hart was not slow to point out.

It's true also that modern audiences tend to be

shown incomplete and mutilated versions of the film, but Cruze's pedestrianism as a director is nevertheless much in evidence. However, the scale of the film, its poetic and evocative theme of the great trek West in 1849, the indisputable visual richness of some scenes such as the river crossing, and above all the impressive photography of Karl Brown, were enough to captivate the audiences of 1923, and without its success much more substantial works such as John Ford's *The Iron Horse* might never have got off the ground.

Cruze followed *The Covered Wagon* in 1925 with *The Pony Express*, but this was a lifeless, unsuccessful affair and had, in any case, been preceded in 1924 by *The Iron Horse*, after *The Covered Wagon* by far the most important of the epics of the twenties, the model for all subsequent railroad Westerns, and a far superior film to *The Covered Wagon* in all respects except photographically.

Ford was twenty-nine when he made *The Iron Horse* and had already directed nearly forty Westerns. His longest film up to that time had been a seven-reeler (about eighty minutes) with John Gilbert called *Cameo Kirby*, which compares with *The Iron Horse*'s two hours and forty minutes, but he was completely the master of his material, not at all cowed by the size or scope of the project he had undertaken. The film has its *longueurs* – few epics escape them – and it contains early signs of Ford's unfortunate taste for slapstick comedy, but it is always alive, smooth-running and packed with activity.

The Iron Horse was made almost wholly on location, and those involved, working under similar conditions to the original pioneer labourers, practically built the Union Pacific railroad all over again! Complete towns were constructed as the unit progressed and a massive train of fifty-six

Left: Raoul Walsh's *The Big Trail* (1930) with John Wayne in his first big starring role. *Right:* Two variations on a popular Western theme, with eleven years separating King Vidor's version of the William Bonney legend (1930, with Johnny Mack Brown in the title role) and David Miller's (1941, with Robert Taylor). Billy the Kid has been played by many other Western actors, including Roy Rogers, Paul Newman, Buster Crabbe, Jack Buetel, Audie Murphy, Scott Brady and Don 'Red' Barry.

coaches was used for transportation. In spite of the film's daunting statistics, however, Ford lost none of his fluency in the making of it; his climactic action scenes in particular, with hordes of Indians attacking one locomotive while another races to the rescue and at the same time hero and villain stage their own personal battle on the side, show Ford's editing skills and fluid camerawork at their best, even at this early stage in a long career.

Ford chose for the lead in this film former assistant cameraman and stuntman George O'Brien, who subsequently became one of the major Western stars of the twenties and thirties, thanks largely to the film's great popular success in America.

Curiously, although they were immensely successful and hold their place of importance in the history of the Western, *The Covered Wagon* and *The Iron Horse* did not inspire an immediate rash of epics as might have been expected. In fact, as the 'B', or series Western began to take a firm grip, and the coming of sound at first discouraged large-scale outdoor film-making, big Westerns became few and far between until the end of the thirties.

Ford made one more silent Western – arguably his best – called *Three Bad Men* (1926), which told a humorous, heroic, mildly tragic tale in best Ford sentimental mood of three rogues with hearts of gold. This appealing work was revived recently after many years on the shelf, and shows itself to be a major Ford film, with excellent playing by character-actors Tom Santschi, Frank Campeau and J. Farrell MacDonald in parts originally intended for Tom Mix, Buck Jones and George O'Brien (though O'Brien was cast in the film in another role). It is also significant in that it marked a thirteen-year pause in Ford's Western output; his next contribution to the genre, in fact, was to be no less a film than *Stagecoach*.

There were other isolated but notable 'quality' Westerns made in the last years of the silent period, and two in particular which stand out as having anticipated the 'psychological' Westerns which became fashionable following *The Ox-Bow Incident* (1943). The first was *White Gold*, made in

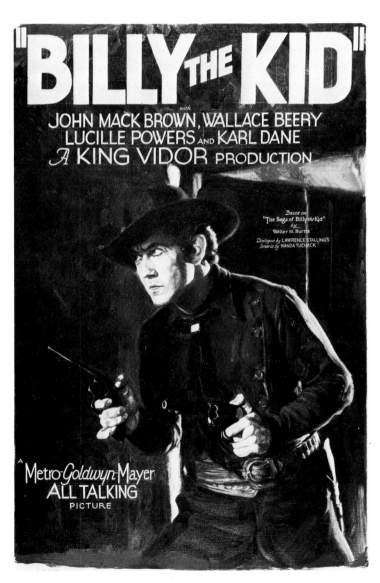

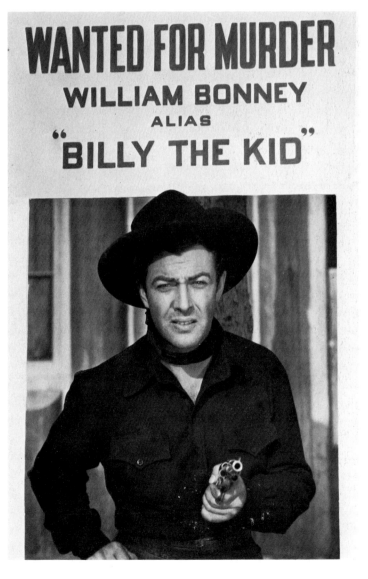

1927 by a highly regarded director of fast-action, melodramatic Westerns, William K. Howard, whose Zane Grey adaptation, *The Thundering Herd* (1925), starring Tim McCoy, Noah Beery and Jack Holt, is best remembered for its extraordinary stampede of covered wagons across a frozen lake. But *White Gold* owed more to the moody, symbolic German art-house imports of the period than to the traditional action Western. Its story of a Mexican dancer who marries and goes to live on a lonely sheep ranch ('white gold' is a euphemism for wool) contained no action and shocked contemporary audiences by killing off the hero (George Bancroft) with a metaphorical shrug of the shoulders – and not surprisingly its box-office appeal proved decidedly limited.

White Gold directly influenced the second of these silent rarities, the similar but more powerful and subtle *The Wind* (1928), directed by the Swedish master Victor Sjöström and containing a vintage Lillian Gish performance. There was one particularly striking scene in which Miss Gish attempts to bury the body of a would-be seducer, whom she has killed, in the midst of a sandstorm.

Remarkable though they were, *White Gold* and *The Wind* were outside the normal run of late-twenties Westerns, and exceptional examples of the genre in what was turning out to be a lean period. Two factors contributed to this depression: Lindbergh's astounding flight across the Atlantic, and the coming of sound. The first of these historic events stole the cowboy's thunder and led to a temporary takeover by a new kind of hero, the seat-of-the-pants aviator. The second led to such an obsession for dialogue and little else that for a while the Western seemed an out-of-date irrelevancy and unsuited to the new technique – though an early Gary Cooper movie, *The Virginian*, directed by Victor Fleming, was partially successful thanks to some excellent playing by Cooper and colleagues Richard Arlen and Walter Huston.

After a year or two of floundering between silent action and static dialogue, the breakthrough came with Raoul Walsh's *In Old Arizona* (1929), a Cisco Kid adventure starring Warner Baxter which took the microphone out of doors and, by picking up gunshots, hoofbeats and natural noises as mundane as the frying of bacon, proved that the Western could more than cope with sound. With the addition of music, particularly traditional Western folk tunes as exploited most effectively later on by such directors as John Ford, the Western's shaky journey into the era of talkies was complete.

Once the genre was sure of itself again, a small cycle of major Westerns gave some distinction to the early thirties before the 'B' boom took over with a vengeance. The first of these was another Raoul Walsh picture, *The Big Trail*, which was made in 1930 and gave John Wayne his first starring role. Unfortunately, apart from a trivial subplot, he was the one inadequate thing in the film, and he remained only a minor star throughout the thirties until *Stagecoach* established the

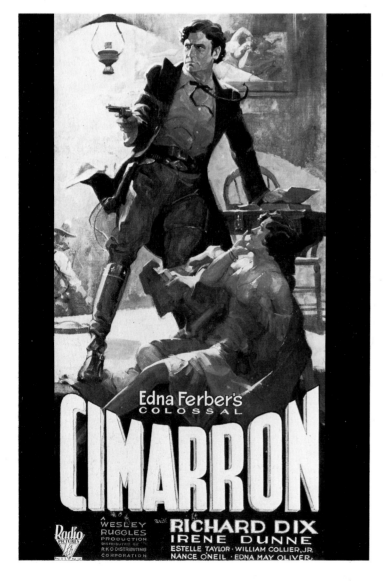

Left: Publicity poster for Wesley Ruggles's *Cimarron* (1931), with an idealized Richard Dix and Irene Dunne on their way to putting Oklahoma on the map of the United States. *Right:* Scenes from the film, including (*above*) the start of the spectacular Cherokee Strip landrush.

special empathy he has enjoyed with John Ford and which has helped turn him into one of the Western's greatest stars.

The Big Trail itself, however, was an impressive piece of work. Originally designed and shown in 70 mm wide-screen, though subsequently exhibited in standard gauge, it depicted the hardships of the great wagon treks in greater detail and far more realistically than *The Covered Wagon*, and contained some brilliantly handled action spectacle in the form of an Indian attack and a buffalo hunt.

King Vidor's *Billy the Kid*, also made in 1930 and also conceived for the then experimental wide-screen, was a slower, more thoughtful affair, concentrating on panorama and long-shot. It recaptured some of the austerity of the old Hart films – not surprisingly since Hart acted as advisor, and coach to the movie's personable young star, Johnny Mack Brown – and generally gave a convincing account of the life of William Bonney, using the actual locations of the Lincoln County wars and stressing the cold-bloodedness of Billy's killings. Certainly none of the numerous subsequent retellings of the story – including Robert Taylor's interpretation of 1941; the fanciful *The Outlaw* (1943); Audie Murphy's version, *The Kid from Texas* (1950); and Arthur Penn's *The Left-Handed Gun* (1958) – has matched it in these respects. Nor has Sheriff Pat Garrett been better played than by Wallace Beery.

The third big Western of the formative sound period, and the most successful commercially, was *Cimarron* (1931). Directed by Wesley Ruggles, it was well played by Richard Dix and Irene Dunne and had a fine sense of scale and good spectacle,

especially in the landrush sequence at the beginning of the film. Latterly it tended to get bogged down in an emotional history of the growth of the state of Oklahoma, but this did not impair its success, nor its influence. Both William Wellman's *The Conquerors* (1932, and again with Richard Dix), and a Mary Pickford/Leslie Howard vehicle, *Secrets* (1933), directed by Frank Borzage, owe their pioneering themes to *Cimarron*.

Two smaller, virtually forgotten, but nevertheless superior Westerns of the period were William Wyler's *Hell's Heroes* (1930), and *Law and Order*, made by Edward L. Cahn in 1932. Like Vidor's *Billy the Kid*, *Law and Order* was an excursion back to the austerity and uncompromising realism of the William Hart movies, achieving a rare atmosphere of tragedy in its story of four lawmen (based on the Earps and Doc Holliday) cleaning up a rough town, and ending in a searing gunfight. Its stars were Walter Huston and Harry Carey, and Andy Devine appeared movingly as an accidental killer whom the lawmen are forced to hang; noteworthy, too, is John Huston's credit as one of the scriptwriters.

After these nuggets, and apart from some glimmerings in 1936, it was not until right at the end of the thirties that the big-production Western began to reassert itself. And from then to the present day the supply has never slackened off. But the yawning gap before 1939 was filled by a product which had grown up in the twenties and carried on through the forties and into the fifties, but which saw its finest hour in the thirties in terms of popularity and prolific output: the 'B' Western.

Prior to *The Covered Wagon* and the subsequent flood of assembly-line Westerns, Hart had been the principal influence on the smaller productions. As Tom Mix grew in popularity, however, and Hart declined, so the studios recognized the potentialities of applying a star system to their Westerns. Most of the major Western stars who grew to popularity in the twenties – Buck Jones, Ken Maynard, Hoot Gibson, Tim McCoy – survived

Above left: Fred Thomson, amiable, athletic star of pre-talkies, in a mid-twenties Western. *Right:* Western exterior set featured as Tombstone in a Fred Thomson picture.

into the thirties. Two exceptions were Fred Thomson, Mix's nearest rival in the silent era, and Art Acord. Hardly anything survives of Acord's work, and he failed to make the transition to sound – but he appears to have had a big popular following behind Mix and Thomson.

Thomson's films took the Mix formula a stage further, emphasizing stunts, action and speed (taken to deliberately comic lengths in the 1924 Fairbanks-inspired *Thundering Hoofs*), strong moral lessons for youngsters (*A Regular Scout*, for example, promoted the cause of the Boy Scouts), and colourful, pristine costume. Thomson died abruptly in 1928.

Apart from the giants, the two Western stars whose work in the twenties has worn well enough to repay viewing half a century later were Buck

Jones and Ken Maynard. Jones retained some roots in the Hart tradition of realism, underplaying and modest costume, but generally followed the Mix formula of straightforward action (such as Scott R. Dunlap's *Good as Gold* of 1925) and light comedy (developed as early as 1920 in John Ford's *Just Pals*, and a pronounced element in, for example, W.S.Van Dyke's 1926 film, *The Gentle Cyclone*).

Maynard was an outstanding stunt rider, who performed all his own tricks, and in his best twenties films he was well served by his productions. They had scale, contained unstinting action and were graced with fine camera-work: so highly esteemed was the action footage from these movies, in fact, that it was constantly pillaged and commercialized to provide highlights for later 'B'

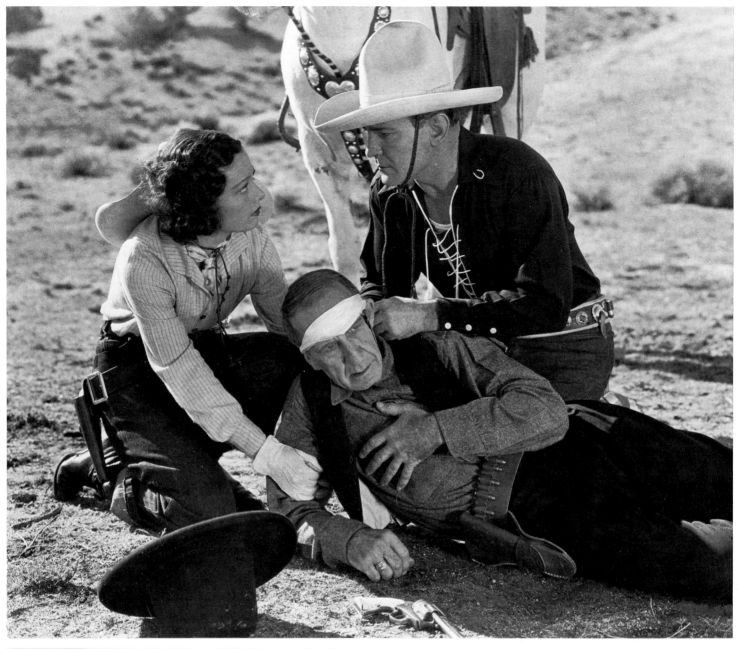

Above and left: Buck Jones in *The Crimson Trail* (1935), with Sally Blane, and *The Ivory-Handled Gun* (1935), directed by Ray Taylor. *Right and far right top:* Ken Maynard in *The Fiddlin' Buckaroo* (1933), which also starred Gloria Shea; and a contemporary Western with 'modern' artefacts, *King of the Arena* (1933), with Bob Kortman and Lucille Brown. *Far right centre:* Colonel Tim McCoy in *Phantom Ranger* (1938), with Karl Hackett. *Far right:* Hoot Gibson (right) and friends taking on the baddies in *The Bearcat* (1922).

Westerns. *Red Raider*, which has occasionally received the accolade of being chosen for cult Western retrospectives in Europe and America, is considered a Maynard film of the highest quality.

Tim McCoy's main output during this period was an interesting series of small-scale historical Westerns, such as *California* (1927) which dealt with the conflict in 1845 between the United States and Mexico – and McCoy achieved a reputation as a more serious Westerner than most. By contrast, Hoot Gibson, an early John Ford discovery (who continued to make appearances for Ford in old age) opted for comedy-action in modern settings, as in *The Texas Streak*.

Another Western star who (or rather which) should not be forgotten from the twenties was Rin Tin Tin, canine hero of *The Night Cry*, perhaps the best of all dog-star movies.

Quantity rather than quality was the feature of the thirties. Maynard and Gibson failed to match their best silent work and found themselves competing with a newer crop of stars such as Johnny Mack Brown and George O'Brien (and two who were serving their apprenticeships to top stardom, John Wayne and Randolph Scott). Buck Jones and Tim McCoy maintained some of their previous high standards, and they were still going strong with a 'Rough Riders' series in 1942 when Jones met a tragic and heroic death while attempting to rescue people trapped in a nightclub fire. But rubbing shoulders with the best work of the Monogram and Republic studios and good, popular series such as Paramount's Zane Grey adaptations,

Above: William Boyd as Clarence E. Mulford's fictional Western hero, Hopalong Cassidy, in one of the first of the series, *The Eagle's Brood* (1935), with Addison Richards. *Far right:* Boyd in *The Devil's Playground* (1946). *Below:* John Wayne replaced Bob Livingston as one of the Three Mesquiteers in 1938; George Sherman directed this example of the immensely successful series.

was a mass of tatty, independent 'quickies' cashing in on the 'B' boom – often so badly made that they perpetrated howlers more glaring than the ill-concealed drain in *The Corporal's Daughter*.

One set of films stands out, however, as a monument to the popularity of the 'B' Western in the thirties – the Hopalong Cassidy series. These began at Paramount in 1935, under the guiding hand of producer Harry Sherman, continued into the forties, and, alongside Gene Autry's musical Westerns, proved to be the most successful 'B' Westerns ever made. Based on Clarence E. Mulford's stories, they stuck to a barely changing formula which was both original and influential. The hero, played by William Boyd, was 'mature' and generally rather inactive, and the plots also tended to inactivity until a sudden burst of climactic action in the last reel, usually a frantic chase backed by tension-building music. In all, Boyd made sixty-six Hopalong Cassidy Westerns, some of the later ones, such as *Forty Thieves* and *Hoppy Serves a Writ*, proving the best.

Also popular for a while was a Republic series devoted to the adventures of 'The Three Mesquiteers', originally starring Ray Corrigan, Bob Livingston and Max Terhune, and later able to count John Wayne among their number. Their hallmark was uncluttered action, with stuntwork arranged and performed by one of Hollywood's greatest stuntmen and second-unit directors, Yakima Canutt. Their settings and plots ranged curiously wide, taking in Nazi spies as well as the early pioneers, but among the best examples were the more conventional *Heart of the Rockies* (1937) and *Outlaws of Sonora* (1938).

Another event of 1935, which was to lead to what many regard as the nadir of the Hollywood Western, was Gene Autry's first big starring vehicle, *Tumbling Tumbleweeds*, which launched the musical Western (and, incidentally, the practice of some stars of using their own names in their film adventures). Ken Maynard had offered a few songs in some of his films, but it was Autry who became established as 'The Singing Cowboy' and one of the top ten moneymakers of his day.

Republic's production standards fortunately lent some quality to Autry's Westerns, notably *Red River Valley* (1936) and *The Yodellin' Kid from Pine Ridge* (1939), and they were deliberately given non-traditional, modern settings. But for some they are best forgotten, particularly as they spawned a vast crop of mostly bad or indifferent imitators, from Tex Ritter and Dick Foran downwards.

Above: Roy Rogers in William Witney's *On the Old Spanish Trail* (1947), with Andy Devine. *Left:* Gene Autry and 'Champion' circa 1940. *Below:* Autry in *Heart of the Rio Grande* (1942). *Right*: Poster for William S. Hart's *Three Word Brand* (1921).

SERVICE

VOL. 5. SAT. FEB. 18 '22. No. 7

WILLIAM S. HART IN
"3 WORD BRAND"
by
WILL REYNOLDS
Adapted and directed by
LAMBERT HILLYER
Photographed by
JOE AUGUST A.S.C.
A WILLIAM S. HART PRODUCTION
A Paramount Picture

The only one to compete on level terms with Autry was the slim, sunny-faced Roy Rogers, owner of the best-known piece of horseflesh of them all, 'Trigger'. While Autry went on eventually to suppress musical content and try his hand at more serious stuff, complete with social comment (*The Last Round-Up*, made in 1947, pointed up the poor lot of the contemporary Indian), Rogers became 'King of the Cowboys' and took the Autry formula even further, with lavish musical production numbers replacing a lot of the action (as in 1944's *The Cowboy and the Senorita*). A

Above: Roy Rogers and 'Trigger' making a guest appearance in Frank Tashlin's *Son of Paleface* (1952). *Left:* Marlon Brando in *One-Eyed Jacks* (1961).

marked feature of the Rogers Westerns was the elaborate, immaculate unisex costumes worn by him and the heroine Dale Evans (later Mrs Roy Rogers); another was the ever-presence of his comic sidekick, George 'Gabby' Hayes, a big improvement on Autry's Smiley Burnette. Latterly, as with Autry, the musical element in

35

Rogers's Westerns was reduced and quite savage action was substituted.

The momentum of the thirties carried the 'B' Western into the forties and a number of veteran stars such as Ken Maynard, Hoot Gibson and Tim McCoy were carried along with it. Monogram revived the 'Cisco Kid' in a decent series with Gilbert Roland, and Johnny Mack Brown made some reasonable tough-action Westerns for the same studio of which Lambert Hillyer's *The Gentleman from Texas* (1946) was a good example.

But by the end of the decade it was clear that the series Western – and the serial, which had reached its peak in 1938 with *The Lone Ranger* – was in a permanent decline, in Hollywood at any rate (many of the present-day European horse operas are a pastiche of the old 'B' Westerns). Production costs had risen and it was no longer possible to make big profits from 'cheap' Westerns since 'cheap' Westerns were no longer possible! And television, of course, finished them off for good in the early fifties.

The 'B' Western's last fling of any merit was, ironically, a harking-back to the traditions of

William S. Hart, the grim-faced good-badman in this case being 'Wild' Bill Elliott. In such films as *Waco* (1952), *Topeka* (1953) and *Bitter Creek* (1954), Elliott displayed a tough realism rather than the good-humoured chivalry of his predecessors – but the quality of his films soon declined.

Some of the more marked characteristics of the 'B' Westerns are worth mentioning before retracing the renaissance of the larger-scale Western. One of these was their strong emphasis on morality, largely as a result of their being aimed at mainly youthful audiences; fair play in particular was stressed, as well as abstinence and respect for women. Gene Autry went so far as to devise 'Ten Commandments of the Cowboy', a code not dissimilar to the Boy Scout law.

Violence was kept to a minimum, not counting fist fights and saloon bust-ups, and blood was hardly ever seen. A fairly ludicrous example of this occurs in a rather poor Ken Maynard vehicle of 1938, *Six Shooting Sheriff*, in which Maynard, shot in the shoulder, goes to great pains to keep the wound away from the camera. In the same film he cleans up a rather tame town with a single shot, bloodlessly wounding the chief villain who clutches his left side – but who, a few seconds later, is seen holding his *right* side, presumably reflecting that if, as the plot demands, he is to survive what he acknowledges to have been 'a fair fight', his wound had better not be too near a vital organ!

Ken Maynard it is, too, who reflects that 'lace curtains and women always did make me nervous', thus speaking for all 'B' Western heroes, whose relationships with women were mostly of the 'Aw, shucks!' variety. Any manifestation of sex was, in any case, unacceptable to the kind of audience these films were aimed at – as anyone who has sat through a screen kiss at a children's Saturday matinée will testify.

As the 'B' Western profited and proliferated in the thirties, the major studios neglected the large-scale Westerns to an unprecedented degree, and it is significant perhaps that even John Ford, as

Above left: Director Fred F. Sears surrounded by the cast of *Apache Ambush* (1955), one of the last gasps of the second-feature Western; from the left, Tex Ritter, Bill Williams, Sears, Cactus Peters, Adelle August, Kermit Maynard (brother of Ken) and Buddy Roosevelt. *Left and right:* Gary Cooper and Jean Arthur (as Calamity Jane) in *The Plainsman* (1936), Cecil B. DeMille's highly romanticized version of the Hickok legend.

noted already, was not offered a single Western until the very end of the period.

There was a very brief revival in 1936, but the films in question, such as William Wellman's biography of the Mexican bandit Joaquin Murietta, *Robin Hood of Eldorado*, are usually referred to as 'interesting' rather than good.

The most 'interesting' was a Universal movie called *Sutter's Gold*, an attempt by James Cruze to make a comeback as a director of epics. The project had an odd history, having been originally designed for the great Russian director Sergei Eisenstein, with English actor Francis L. Sullivan as star. Howard Hawks directed a few scenes before Cruze took over, and Edward Arnold was given the starring role as the Swiss immigrant who discovered gold in California. Unfortunately, Cruze was even less at home with sound epics than he had been with silent – in fact, so unsure was his handling of an unwieldy, episodic story that he frequently resorted to subtitles to push the plot

along. Commercially the film was a disaster, and the studio was saved only by its timely and marvellous James Whale musical, *Show Boat*.

Paramount, the most 'epic-minded' producers at this period, came up with a more conventional piece in *The Plainsman*, a highly romanticized account of the life and death of Wild Bill Hickok. Cecil B. DeMille directed and Gary Cooper starred, while Calamity Jane, in the unlikely person of Jean Arthur, and Buffalo Bill (James Ellison) were thrown in for good measure. It's a showy film, full of DeMille's weakness for fancy dress and corny lines, and rather studio-bound, but likeable nevertheless, and well played by a most attractive cast.

Another Paramount movie, *The Texas Rangers*, also suffered from trite dialogue, but director King Vidor's gift for spectacle and action lifted it out of the rut, and it was well served by an interesting cast which included Jack Oakie, Fred MacMurray and Lloyd Nolan.

In 1937 Paramount tried again with *Wells Fargo*,

Below: Joel McCrea and Barbara Stanwyck receive close attention from Anthony Quinn and Lynne Overman in DeMille's blockbuster of 1939, *Union Pacific. Right:* The lull before the shoot-out climax of *Stagecoach* (1939), with Claire Trevor as Dallas and John Wayne as Ringo.

Joel McCrea starring and Frank Lloyd directing, but its historical portentousness and dull pace undermined the potentialities of its epic theme and it did badly. Also unsuccessful was the fourth Paramount venture of the period, *The Texans* (1938), which starred Randolph Scott and Joan Bennett in a cattle-drive story with rather conventional direction from James Hogan. But the years of famine for Western-hungry audiences were about to end.

While John Ford's *Stagecoach* is rightly singled out as the film which re-established the viability of the main-feature Western and began the renaissance which has yet to show signs of diminishing, the year of its production, 1939, was a particularly rich one for all varieties of the Western film.

The blockbuster of the year was *Union Pacific* – virtually a remake of *The Iron Horse* but more attentive to its empire-building theme, and one of DeMille's best films. It was also timely in that the Depression was ending and the war in Europe impending, and the American people were ready again to take pride in the kind of national progress represented by such a theme as the building of the Union Pacific railroad.

DeMille's naive flag-waving and special brand of corn still show through in this film, particularly in the mawkish ending after weak-but-good Robert Preston has died after saving hero Joel McCrea's life; but the action is constant and unstinting, taking in Indian attacks, a saloon-wrecking fight, a train smash in a snowbound canyon, a hold-up and a shoot-out finale, and whatever its faults, it remains a big and exciting Western.

Stagecoach: John Ford's first use of his favourite location (*right*), Monument Valley, Utah. *Above:* Preparing for the Indian attack; John Wayne, Louise Platt.

Above: An early spoof, *Go West* (1925) with Buster Keaton. *Right and below: Destry Rides Again* (1939), George Marshall's revival of the comedy Western, with Marlene Dietrich watching the bullying of Charles Winninger and taking aim at James Stewart.

Yet it was the less ambitious *Stagecoach* which was to exert more influence on the genre than probably any Western before or since. It was the first Western to combine successfully the poetic grandeur and sense of myth-making of the real and imaginary West with pure entertainment values – and most importantly it was literate enough (having its roots in de Maupassant's 'Boule de Suif', no less) to inspire big-name stars to regard the Western as equally worthy of their attention as any serious modern drama or classical adaptation.

Everything seems to click in *Stagecoach* from the very first moment that the camera races in on the imposing figure of John Wayne, clad in unfashionable braces and twirling his Winchester rifle in one hand. The fabulous Monument Valley location, used here by Ford for the first time, seems no longer to dwarf the coachful of assorted characters now that they have a man among them who fits into such scenery, and it's clear that, when the Indian attack comes, Geronimo will have a fight on his hands.

The famous chase across the salt flats, sparked off by the genuine shock-effect of an arrow thudding into Donald Meek's shoulder, was criticized by William S. Hart on the grounds that the Indians

would have been smart enough to shoot the horses first – a cavil dismissed with characteristic blunt logic by Ford who pointed out that had they done so, that would have been the end of the film! The remarkable thing is that this magnificent highlight, staged brilliantly by second-unit director and stunt organizer Yakima Canutt, does not overshadow the gunfight finale, which is handled with wit as well as suspense.

Remarkable also, but not so surprising in the light of Ford's subsequent handling of character interplay, is the fact that the aurorean presence of Wayne is not allowed to interfere with the intelligent playing of Claire Trevor, Thomas Mitchell, John Carradine, Meek, George Bancroft, Andy Devine *et al.*

Stagecoach is a key film not only in the careers of John Ford (it was his first sound Western) and John Wayne (whom it rescued from nine years of 'B' picture-making), but in the history of the Western genre also. It was, as they say, the start of something big. (A 1966 remake, incidentally, should be given a wide berth.)

Ford followed *Stagecoach* in the same year with another fine Western, *Drums Along the Mohawk*, in which he used Henry Fonda for the first time. This was a film dedicated to the pioneer spirit, a favourite Ford theme, as it told of the tribulations of a young couple trying to settle down in the rugged early days of the West. It had humour (pointed up by the playing of Claudette Colbert), excitement (including a memorably original sequence in which Fonda outruns two Indians to bring help to a besieged fort), and a delightfully tetchy, no-truck-with-the-Indians performance by Edna May Oliver.

Many aficionados regard *Drums Along the Mohawk* as one of the great Westerns, and it certainly features on many people's list of favourites. The same goes for two more major Westerns produced in the extraordinary year of '39, the way-out *Destry Rides Again* and the ultra-traditional *The Oklahoma Kid*, neither of which has lost its popularity or appeal over the years.

Destry Rides Again was a revival of the spoof Western, which had virtually lain dormant since the satires of Mack Sennett and the kidding of Douglas Fairbanks in the twenties, and it has remained one of the most successful. Directed with verve by George Marshall, it has a crop of witty lines expertly delivered by a youthful James Stewart as a pacifist sheriff, some of the best barroom scenes in any Western, an excellent musical score by Frank Skinner, and one of Brian Donlevy's

most endearingly treacherous 'heavy' performances. Above all, though, it has Marlene Dietrich, transferring her 'Blue Angel' sexuality to the wild frontier, devastating cowboy and audience alike with her inimitable rendering of 'See What the Boys in the Back Room Will Have', and retaining her allure even at the end of an unladylike brawl with Una Merkel when both have been drenched with water.

The fact that *Destry Rides Again* was, and is, so acceptable and enjoyable as a spoof on the Western is in itself remarkable, since very few other attempts have been even half as successful. Of the Western vehicles specifically designed for comedians – *Buck Benny Rides Again* (Jack Benny), *Paleface*, *Fancy Pants* and *Son of Paleface* (Bob Hope), *Pardners* (Dean Martin and Jerry Lewis), *Ride 'Em Cowboy* (Bud Abbott and Lou Costello), *Go West* (Marx Brothers), etc. – only the last-named and to some extent *Paleface* really hit the mark; while of more recent efforts, only Burt Kennedy's *Support Your Local Sheriff* really works, and even *Cat Ballou* would be nothing without Lee Marvin's Oscar-winning performance.

The Oklahoma Kid, in spite of being a starring vehicle for protagonists James Cagney and Humphrey Bogart and tackling an epic theme,

The Western played for laughs, with Jane Fonda (*left*) as *Cat Ballou* (1965), aided and opposed by Lee Marvin (*below left and centre*) in his Oscar-winning dual role; cross-eyed Ben Turpin (*below*) in an early piece of satire featured in Robert Youngson's *Days of Thrills and Laughter* (1961); Bob Hope and Lucille Ball (*right*) in *Fancy Pants* (1950), directed by George Marshall, and Hope again (*below right and far right*) in *Son of Paleface* (1952), with Roy Rogers; and (*below right centre*) Harpo in the Marx Brothers' *Go West* (1940).

moved at the speed of a 'B' Western and stuck to such traditional fast-action elements as fist fights and horseback rides. In fact, the film's one epic moment, yet another reconstruction of the Cherokee Strip landrush, is among the tamest of the cinema's many depictions of this event, and it is virtually thrown away while Cagney and old-timer Donald Crisp hold a polemical conversation about the virtues or otherwise of law and order ('This is the *only* law,' says Cagney, patting his six-shooter – as if the plot would ever tolerate any other conclusion).

Cagney, as a cocky, wise-cracking good-badman (more or less his city gangster character in cow-poke's clothing), and Bogart, as the humourless, black-clad villain, Whip McCord, provide the film's best moments when they are sharing the screen – notably in a marvellous bar-room scene during which henchman Ward Bond has interrupted Cagney's rendering of 'I Don't Wanna Play in Your Yard, I Don't Like You Any More' at the saloon piano and received a bloody nose for his trouble. Bogart introduces himself to Cagney. 'McCord, McCord,' muses Cagney, 'I don't like it . . .' (and turning to the pianist, who is semi-paralysed with fright) '. . . how about you?' The pianist, in a moment of pure cinema joy, starts to shake his head in agreement, and then, spotting Bogart's hostile glare, slowly turns the shake into a sheepish nod.

Such moments are what *The Oklahoma Kid* is all about and why it is still a Western to cherish. This is one of the few films, incidentally, where it is possible actually to see the so-called cliché of a man blowing the smoke from the barrel of his six-gun after he has fired it.

Another major Western of 1939 began a new vogue for romanticizing the West's real outlaws.

This was Henry King's *Jesse James*, which did at least keep one foot on the straight and narrow path of historical fact, although allowing Tyrone Power to over-indulge his interpretation of Jesse as a handsome, noble, charming, ill-fated and misunderstood Robin Hood of the West. The real Jesse probably had a few genuine grievances, but he was a hard killer nevertheless.

Distortions apart, King's film contains many excellent features, not least an authentic setting beautifully photographed in Technicolor, and an impressive, upstaging performance by Henry Fonda as brother Frank (whom he played again a year later in Fritz Lang's sequel, *The Return of Frank James*). There is, too, an outstanding bank robbery sequence in which, prevented from making a getaway by wagons shunted across each end of the street, Jesse and Frank escape by riding through a shop window while their colleagues panic and tumble from their mounts.

It says something for the film's qualities that when Nicholas Ray made *The True Story of Jesse James* (in Britain, *The James Brothers*) in 1957, with Robert Wagner and Jeffrey Hunter in the main parts, he stuck closely to King's version of the legend.

Jesse James was followed by *When the Daltons Rode* (1940), *Badmen of Missouri* (1941, with Arthur Kennedy, Dennis Morgan and Wayne Morris as the Younger Brothers), David Miller's version of *Billy the Kid* (1941), and then a rather silly string of hybrids featuring any combination of known badmen with (usually) Randolph Scott striving to keep order behind his marshal's badge.

When the Daltons Rode, which was directed by George Marshall and starred Randolph Scott, with Broderick Crawford in support as one of the Daltons, was distinguished by a celebrated train

Left and far left: James Cagney as *The Oklahoma Kid* (1939), directed by Lloyd Bacon, with Ward Bond and a black-clad Humphrey Bogart. *Right and below:* Two versions of the James legend — Henry King's *Jesse James* (1939), with Henry Fonda and Tyrone Power, and Nicholas Ray's *The True Story of Jesse James* (1957), which starred Robert Wagner and Jeffrey Hunter as the outlaw brothers.

hold-up sequence, and, historical inaccuracies apart, generally came off better than the pretentious remake of *Billy the Kid*. Robert Taylor was far too virile and mature in the name part, and a ludicrous ending has the Kid deliberately inviting death by allowing Sheriff Pat Garrett (Brian Donlevy) to beat him to the draw, following which he sinks to the ground with a satisfied smile on his face!

One of the results of the success of *Union Pacific* was a proliferation of historical Westerns, often as vehicles for big stars. DeMille himself followed up with *Northwest Mounted Police* (1940), a crashingly dull picture with minimal action not even redeemed by a cast which included Gary Cooper, Madeleine Carroll, Robert Preston, Paulette Goddard and Preston Foster, but before this Errol Flynn had begun an interesting excursion into Westerns with *Dodge City* (1939), a simple, archetypal town-taming movie with plenty of action and slick direction by Michael Curtiz.

Two more Curtiz/Flynn films followed in 1940 – *Virginia City*, with a fast-moving Civil War gold robbery plot, Randolph Scott as co-star and

Humphrey Bogart as (Mexican) villain; and *Santa Fé Trail*, an honest reconstruction of John Brown's pro-slave rebellion culminating in the battle at Harper's Ferry, with Raymond Massey as Brown – and then in 1941 Flynn impersonated General Custer for Raoul Walsh in *They Died with Their Boots On*. This ranged widely and somewhat inaccurately over the Civil War, its aftermath and the growing hostility between whites and Indians, culminating in a decently staged Last Stand. Thereafter Errol Flynn's few Westerns declined rather sadly, apart from a brief revival in *San Antonio*.

Zane Grey's WESTERN UNION in TECHNICOLOR

with ROBERT YOUNG ★ RANDOLPH SCOTT ★ DEAN JAGGER ★ VIRGINIA GILMORE AND John CARRADINE SUMMERVILLE Slim Chill WILLS Barton McLANE DIRECTED BY FRITZ LANG Harry Joe Brown ASSOCIATE PRODUCER A 20th CENTURY ·FOX PICTURE SCREEN PLAY BY ROBERT CARSON

Other historical Westerns of this period included two re-teamings of John Wayne and Claire Trevor – in Walsh's *The Dark Command*, an account of Quantrell's guerilla raiders, and the unsuccessful *Allegheny Uprising*; Wesley (*Cimarron*) Ruggles's *Arizona*, a panoramic, logistically impressive, but static and dull account of the growth of the state; *Texas*, a much livelier movie under George Marshall's direction; and in 1944, *Buffalo Bill*, a sentimental affair directed by William Wellman which starred Joel McCrea as Bill Cody and contained a spectacular cavalry v. Indians battle staged in the middle of a river. Far more effective as a film biography, however, had been *Man of Conquest* (1939), Richard Dix's interpretation of Texas's greatest hero, Sam Houston, with San Jacinto battle scenes (staged by old hands Yakima Canutt and Reeves Eason) which have received more than favourable comparison with John Wayne's for *The Alamo*. One of the best of this crop of historical movies, in a traditional sense, was Fritz Lang's second Western, *Western Union* (1941), which recounted the construction of the telegraph system and souped up a dull story with Indian attacks, a forest fire and outlaws (chiefly Randolph Scott – far more colourful than heroes Robert Young and Dean Jagger). The film was not, incidentally, 'Zane Grey's *Western Union*' as advertised at the time – that was just one of Hollywood's little white lies!

Early forties Westerns were not entirely devoted to badman biographies and historical reconstructions, and a number of interesting and offbeat films were being added to the genre. William

Above left: The teaming of director Michael Curtiz and star Errol Flynn produced two exciting Westerns in 1940 – *Virginia City*, with Humphrey Bogart, and *Santa Fé Trail*, with Olivia de Havilland. Flynn also appeared as General Custer (*centre left*) in Raoul Walsh's *They Died with Their Boots On* (1941). *Below left:* Indians on the warpath in William Wellman's *Buffalo Bill* (1944). *Above:* Poster for *Western Union* (1941), erroneously attributing it to Zane Grey. *Below:* Virginia Gilmore salutes the transcontinental telegraph in *Western Union*.

Wyler's *The Westerner*, made in 1940 and starring Gary Cooper, was an unusually serious, restrained, naturalistic and austere re-creation of the West, with an outstanding character performance by Walter Brennan as the notorious Judge Roy Bean (later exploited in a television series). The film's moodiness anticipated the later fashion for more introverted Westerns, while its fights reverted right back to the more realistic clumsy brawls of the early silent days.

Two Harry Sherman productions starring Joel McCrea later in the decade echoed the austerity of *The Westerner: Ramrod* (1947), directed by André de Toth, a tense, range-war Western, and Alfred E. Green's *Four Faces West* (1948), with McCrea as an outlaw on the run. More conventionally entertaining, however, had been *The Spoilers* (1942), which put John Wayne, Randolph Scott, Marlene Dietrich, Richard Barthelmess, Harry Carey and William Farnum all on the same screen, and provided one of the biggest slam-bang fight climaxes ever.

In among the multiplication of major Westerns which spelled out the genre's revival in the first half of the forties were three which have a special significance in that they signposted the main new trends of the fifties and after: *The Ox-Bow Incident*, *The Outlaw* (both 1943) and *Duel in the Sun* (1945).

The Ox-Bow Incident (retitled *Strange Incident* in Britain) is sometimes called the first 'psychological' Western, which of course is inaccurate since many serious Westerns prior to it had attempted to probe the psyche. What is probably meant is that it was the first Western to show a deep, uncompromising social conscience; to tackle a serious, controversial theme in a literate way without once resorting to conventional escapist trappings; and to delve into the minds and motives of a variety of non-stock, unheroic characters confronted with a situation outside their normal experience.

The film is an indictment of lynching, somewhat studio-bound but nevertheless powerfully expressed through William Wellman's stark direction. A posse of ranchers and drifters pursues a

Top left: Gregory Peck in Wellman's *Yellow Sky* (1948). *Left and above left:* Wellman's major Western contribution, *The Ox-Bow Incident* (1943), a stark, uncompromising indictment of lynch law, with Henry Fonda, Frank Conroy, Anthony Quinn and Dana Andrews. *Right:* Burt Lancaster and Audrey Hepburn in John Huston's *The Unforgiven* (1960).

gang of cattle thieves and captures a trio of suspects (Dana Andrews, Anthony Quinn, Francis Ford) of whose possible guilt there is circumstantial evidence. The men swear that they can prove their innocence within a few hours, but the posse's leader, an ex-Confederate army officer, speaks eloquently for their immediate execution and the men are hanged. Proof of their innocence duly arrives, and the sadistic army man commits suicide because of the dishonour his mistake will bring him.

This grim tale is peopled with a cross-section of the humane, the cold-blooded, the weak and the ordinary (even the film's 'star', Henry Fonda, acting more as a sympathetic observer than as a hero) and after *Ox-Bow*, introspection became an indispensable part of many Westerners' character

Right: William Wyler's *The Westerner* (1940), with Gary Cooper, Walter Brennan and Lilian Bond. *Below: The Spoilers* (1942) with Marlene Dietrich, Richard Barthelmess and John Wayne. *Left:* Paul Newman and Robert Redford cornered in *Butch Cassidy and the Sundance Kid* (1969).

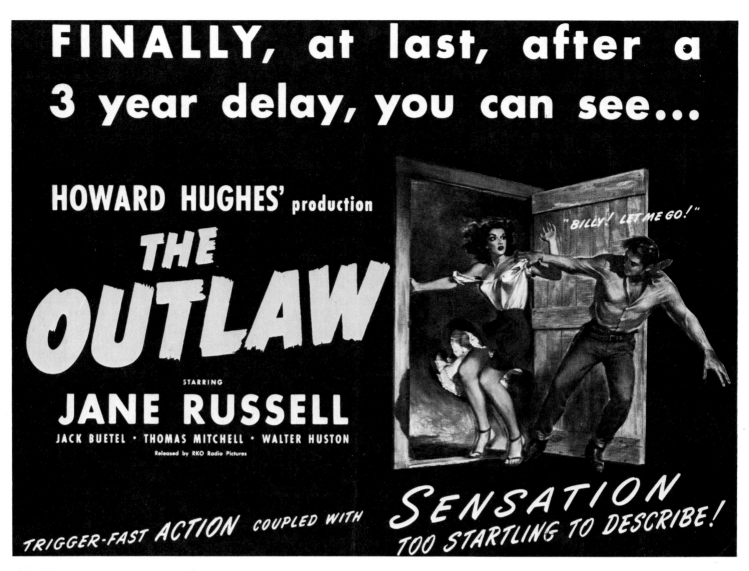

FINALLY, at last, after a 3 year delay, you can see...

HOWARD HUGHES' production

THE OUTLAW

STARRING

JANE RUSSELL

JACK BUETEL · THOMAS MITCHELL · WALTER HUSTON

Released by RKO Radio Pictures

"BILLY! LET ME GO!"

TRIGGER-FAST ACTION COUPLED WITH

SENSATION TOO STARTLING TO DESCRIBE!

make-up, and social comment (or 'message') a *sine qua non* of many a Western plot. Even quite conventional movies such as *Yellow Sky* (1948 – Wellman again, with Gregory Peck as star) and the melancholic, fatalistic *Colorado Territory* (1949 – Raoul Walsh, with Joel McCrea) caught the *Ox-Bow* flavour and benefited from its addition to their more traditional aims.

The Outlaw was the first blatant manifestation of a quite different influence that was to exert itself in Westerns from the forties onwards: sex. As had been more than hinted at in *Destry Rides Again*, women in Westerns were about to cease to be simply objects of respect and potential mother-hood, to be saved from time to time from a fate worse than death at the hands of a dark villain or a savage Indian – life on the open range was about to become a little more earthy. The woman chosen

by Howard Hughes to effect this revolution – and chosen more for her physical attributes than her histrionic ability – was Jane Russell. Hughes went so far as to design a special enhancing bra for Miss Russell's ample bosom, and it is true that, as the critics and censors of the time pointed out, in her role as Rio she is intended principally as an object of lust and little else. In fact, when it comes to the crunch, she is adjudged to be far less useful than a horse!

As a Western rather than as a study in eroticism, *The Outlaw* has some merits, though it is often banal and gratuitously sadistic. It is yet another variation of the Billy the Kid story, showing even less regard for accuracy than usual by bringing in Doc Holliday as a protagonist and allowing Billy (accompanied by Rio) to ride off at the end scot-free. On the credit side, Jack Buetel, though not much of an actor, at least made Billy a refreshingly and more realistically unpleasant character than has been customary, while veterans Walter Huston (as Holliday) and Thomas Mitchell (as Billy's pursuer, Sheriff Pat Garrett) gave satisfyingly wry, rounded performances.

The action, mostly in the form of gun-duels, was extremely well handled, for once making Billy's draws look genuinely fast and deadly – and the film contains at least one extraordinary and memorable scene, in which (and it's not quite as nasty in context as it sounds) Doc is forced to shoot notches in Billy's ears in order to provoke the younger man into drawing his gun.

The Outlaw fell foul of the censors and its release was delayed while minor concessions were made (marrying Billy to Rio somewhere off-screen, for example). But Hughes had paved the way for passion, and it only needed someone to make it respectable.

This King Vidor did in *Duel in the Sun* (or 'Lust in the Dust' as it came to be known), which featured a torrid love affair between lecherous Gregory Peck and sensual half-breed Jennifer Jones against an epic background of empire-building. The film's size, production gloss, quality

Above left: After some hesitation, sex finally comes to the Western. *Far left:* The unmistakable Jane Russell as she appeared in *The Outlaw* (1943). *Left and above right:* More sex, but less blatantly packaged, in King Vidor's *Duel in the Sun* (1945), with Jennifer Jones and Gregory Peck as the lovers. *Right:* Walter Huston as Doc Holliday and Jack Buetel as Billy the Kid in *The Outlaw*.

cast (including Lillian Gish, Herbert Marshall, Joseph Cotten, Harry Carey) and obvious merits helped it to overcome censorship difficulties and it became a huge box-office success. Its use of colour and dramatic lighting effects was particularly imaginative, and Vidor stirred memories of his earlier days with a mass-riding sequence in which ranchers gather to oppose the intruding railroad.

The sex scenes now look a little overplayed and faintly risible at times, especially the lovers' climactic passionate suicide pact, but they have an erotic power none the less, while Vidor's innate sense of style on the grand scale carries the film over any inconsistencies it might have.

A man who had worked with Hughes on *The Outlaw* suddenly came to prominence in 1948 as a director (and producer) of Westerns: Howard Hawks. The film in question was *Red River* which, at the time, seemed something like the ultimate in the Western film. Hawks, a veteran who directed his first feature in 1926, has become a cult figure among serious critics in recent years. His output includes social satire, aviation melodrama, motor-racing – and four major Westerns, one of which, *Rio Bravo*, is deservedly recognized as a classic (a fifth Western, his latest, *Rio Lobo*, is a pale pastiche of *Rio Bravo* and shows a marked decline in Hawks's powers).

Red River was the first of Hawks's major Westerns and remains his biggest. Conceived on an epic scale, and with a story spread over twenty years, its principal action is a cattle drive and its

theme the conflict and love-hate relationship of two men – one, the ruthless leader of the drive (John Wayne), who handles his men with a bullwhip, and the other a cowboy (Montgomery Clift) who rebels against his methods. It is, in effect, a Western version of *Mutiny on the Bounty*, the main difference being that *Red River* ends with the chief protagonists professing mutual admiration after a furious fist-fight and a brandishing of firearms.

Red River hardly merits the amount of analysis and reappraisal it has undergone following the critics' discipleship of Hawks, but it did reinstate the epic Western after a brief lull, and it installed Hawks immediately as Ford's principal rival among directors of Westerns, though their styles and attitudes are in complete contrast: Ford the poet, the sentimentalist; Hawks the anti-romantic.

The late forties was in fact the period when John Ford made his most endearing, idyllic and optimistic Westerns, culminating in the best loved of them all, *Wagonmaster*.

My Darling Clementine, made in 1946, was the first product of this purple patch – and Ford's first Western since 1939 (though he had of course been making other films meanwhile, notably *The Grapes of Wrath* and *How Green Was My Valley*). It was Ford's version of the Wyatt Earp story, superficially a remake of the 1939 *Frontier Marshal* (which had Randolph Scott as Earp and Cesar Romero as Doc Holliday), and a strange but haunting mixture of fact (the climactic gunfight at the OK Corral is a careful reconstruction of the actual

Left: Howard Hawks's *Red River* (1948), with (*top*) the cattle drovers repulsing an Indian attack, (*centre*) John Wayne beating John Ireland to the draw, and (*bottom*) Wayne with Montgomery Clift. *Above and below: My Darling Clementine* (1946), first product of John Ford's richest period of Western film-making, a warm and idiosyncratic version of the Earp legend with Henry Fonda as Wyatt Earp and Victor Mature as the consumptive Doc Holliday.

Left and below: Two more versions of the Earp legend, both by John Sturges – *Gunfight at the OK Corral* (1957), with Kirk Douglas (as Doc Holliday) and Jo van Fleet, and *Hour of the Gun* (1967), with James Garner as Wyatt Earp (right) and Jason Robards Jnr as Doc Holliday (with shotgun). *Right: Fort Apache* (1948), John Ford's first cavalry Western, with George O'Brien (left), Shirley Temple, John Wayne and Henry Fonda. *Far right and bottom right: She Wore a Yellow Ribbon* (1949), with John Wayne. *Centre right:* Two scenes from *Wagonmaster* (1950), with Ben Johnson, Joanne Dru, Harry Carey Jnr, Ward Bond and (in top hat) Alan Mowbray.

confrontation, described to a much younger Ford by Earp himself) and Ford's own poetic vision of how life in the rugged days of a frontier town like Tombstone must have been.

On a purely historical level it is a much better Earp film than the overblown *Gunfight at the OK Corral* made in 1957 with Burt Lancaster and Kirk Douglas, though less attentive to facts and the probable truer character of Earp than the savage, serious *Hour of the Gun* (1967), with James Garner a ruthless, vengeance-seeking Earp and Jason Robards Jnr a reflective, world-weary Holliday. Henry Fonda's marvellous characterization of Earp in *Clementine* is, by contrast, pure Ford – shy, gauche and peace-loving, but quietly determined to create a West fit for decent family folk to live in.

And it is a nice Ford touch that, at the very end, Earp rides away from his Clementine, acknowledging that the job is still not yet done.

Where *Clementine* almost breaks down is in its representation of the consumptive Doc Holliday (a Byronic, smouldering Victor Mature coughing incessantly into a Persil-white handkerchief) and the over-presence of anachronistic Linda Darnell (a forties chick if ever there was one) as Doc's woman. But they are both part of Ford's romantic concept, and easily offset by the murderous Clantons, led by a whining, indignant Walter Brennan.

This is certainly one of John Ford's most beautiful films – rich in its observation of human foibles and period detail and beautifully photographed in black and white by Joseph P. MacDonald.

Ford followed *Clementine* in 1948 with two more Westerns: *Fort Apache*, the first of his cavalry films, with Henry Fonda unsympathetically cast for once as a martinet lieutenant-colonel nursing a blind hate for the Indian and leading his men into an Apache massacre; and the frequently filmed *Three Godfathers*, a slight work but a very personal one since it was made as a dedication to Harry Carey, one of the old, enduring Western stars ('. . . bright star of the early Western sky'), a favourite of Ford's who had died the year before. The cast contained John Wayne, Harry Carey Jnr, Pedro Armendariz, and many more veterans and Ford favourites including Ward Bond, Jane Darwell, Mae Marsh, Ben Johnson and Francis Ford (John's brother).

Then in 1949 Ford made his second cavalry film – and the most sentimental of all his Westerns – *She Wore a Yellow Ribbon*. Many disciples quote this as their favourite Ford film, and it is certainly his most lyrical and among the most striking visually (Ford styled it on the works of Remington, one of the great artists of the American West, and Winton C. Hoch won an Oscar for his Technicolor photography). The story is that of an ageing cavalry officer (John Wayne) staving off his impending retirement, and his last mission before that inevitable day comes. Action quite rightly takes second place to this simple theme, and the film is full of Ford's best touches – the comic by-play between old-stagers Wayne and Victor McLaglen, the rivalry of two young cavalry lieutenants (John Agar and Harry Carey Jnr) for the attentions of the girl with the yellow ribbon (Joanne Dru), and the evocative use of music (notably the title song).

Ford has made it a policy of his film-making to slip the occasional modest, personal, non-com-

The predicament of the North American Indian receiving rare recognition in (*above*) Delmer Daves's *Broken Arrow* (1950), with James Stewart; (*below*) John Ford's epic *Cheyenne Autumn* (1964); (*above right*) Zane Grey's *The Vanishing American* (1926), directed by George B. Seitz as a mixture of melodrama, liberal propaganda and straight documentary, and beautifully shot in Monument Valley; and (*right*) Arthur Penn's *Little Big Man* (1970), with Dustin Hoffman.

mercial movie into his more ambitious output – a film he might just want to make for its own sake, a form of therapy – and these have often proved to be among his best. Such a film is *Wagonmaster*, a small (less than ninety minutes long), black and white, positively old-fashioned homage to the pioneer spirit, which has that rare quality in a film of seeming to gain in stature and appeal with every viewing. Crammed with traditional Western songs rendered by The Sons of the Pioneers, it tells of the trek West to Utah of a Mormon wagon train led by two young horse traders (Ben Johnson and Harry Carey Jnr). And in a series of beautiful images, as

the wagon train fights outlaws, Indians and nature in its struggle to reach the promised land, the modest *Wagonmaster* manages to capture more of the history and legend of the West than a dozen epics from *The Covered Wagon* onwards.

Ford himself has said that *Wagonmaster* – of which he wrote the original story – was among the three films of his which 'came closest to being what I had wanted to achieve'.

Ford followed *Wagonmaster* in 1950 with the third of his cavalry Westerns, *Rio Grande*, a gentle study of the reconciliation of a colonel (John Wayne) and his estranged wife (Maureen O'Hara) during their involvement in the Apache wars. Then there was another pause in his Western output until 1956, when *The Searchers* introduced a tougher, less optimistic John Ford.

Meanwhile, 1950 was proving to be a significant year for the Western film. Anthony Mann emerged as a director worth watching with *The Devil's Doorway*, *The Furies* and the better-known *Winchester '73* – thus commencing a decade of memorable Westerns with a predominantly violent theme, and an equally memorable partnership with James Stewart. Another newcomer to the genre, Delmer Daves, directed a key film in Hollywood's attitudes to the American Indian, *Broken Arrow*. And old

hand Henry King came up with an inspired and ultimately highly influential movie, *The Gunfighter*, which has had an effect on practically all so-called 'psychological' Westerns made subsequently.

Until *Broken Arrow* the Indian had received scant sympathy from the Western film-maker, apart from some silent movies (notably by Thomas Ince) which presented him in an idealized but nevertheless alien form (the 'noble savage'), and

occasional enlightened forties films (e.g. *She Wore a Yellow Ribbon*) which ventured to suggest that he might have been hard done by. In between he had been treated dispassionately and remotely as six-gun fodder, a natural hazard to the pioneer and dispensable in great numbers.

Certainly no film had dared to suggest that the Red Indian could be as kind, considerate and *human* as the white man, with a way of life which might be just as acceptable as the white man's. *Broken Arrow* did all this (and in so doing paved the way for a continual re-examination ever since of the treatment of the American Indian by enlightened film-makers) and contrived also to be a fine Western in its own right, beautifully photographed, and written and directed by Daves with obvious sincerity.

The film introduced Jeff Chandler in his first major part as Cochise, the Apache chief, and James Stewart played the white man who befriends him and marries an Indian girl (Debra Paget). Having gone so far in exposing the grievances of the Indians and their exploitation, it is a little disappointing that the film compromises in the end by killing off Debra Paget so that the mixed marriage cannot survive and the couple 'live happily ever after'. But films with a racial theme were still treading carefully in 1950.

In recent years, of course, film-makers have become completely outspoken in their condemnation of what has almost amounted to genocide – tragically in *Cheyenne Autumn*, repulsively in *Soldier Blue*, and both lyrically and ironically in *Little Big Man*. But *Broken Arrow*, although its attitude now may seem a little cautious and its portrait of the Indian rather 'tasteful' (the main Apache protagonists are, after all, played by attractive white stars), does represent a considerable breakthrough for the Indian Western.

The Gunfighter, a dark, tragic, brooding film, remains a classic Western, the first of any consequence to present the now-familiar theme of the mature outlaw unable to settle down and live in peace because of the young punk in every town ready to call him out in the hope of killing him and making a name for himself. The irony, of course, being that the older man's problem is thus inherited by the young punk.

In King's hands – and thanks in no small measure to a performance of restraint and rare quality from Gregory Peck as the gunfighter – this theme takes on an air of Greek tragedy, and the neat trick is achieved of making the audience sympathize with the character who ought morally to be regarded as the most reprehensible: one of the first manifestations of the anti-hero.

The Gunfighter, a misunderstood and commercially unsuccessful film, has by and large been forgotten by the mainstream filmgoer, and it remains unluckily and unjustifiably a 'connoisseur's piece'. Yet it has exerted considerable influence on the 'adult' Western – and significantly there are strong elements of its mood and character in the film, made in 1952, which is regarded by many as *the* representative post-war Western, and the one with which the genre finally came of age: Fred Zinnemann's *High Noon*.

The classical shape, somewhat contrived format and taut theme of *High Noon* have been copied many times since, most closely in *3.10 to Yuma*, in which Van Heflin, like Gary Cooper, finds himself standing alone and outnumbered against the villains. *High Noon* was made in the climate of the McCarthy witch-hunt in America, and much of its critical acclaim has accrued from the way in which its theme has been interpreted as an allegory of those dark days (Carl Foreman, a victim of the McCarthy purge in Hollywood who left America to live in Britain, was the film's scriptwriter). In so far as it is about fear, civic responsibility and the courage of the individual prepared to fight victimization, the analogy is valid – but it is also an outstanding Western in other ways.

The build-up of tension as the lawman (Cooper) prepares to meet the villains and makes fruitless attempts to recruit help from the panic-ridden townsfolk has never been handled better, and (unlike *3.10 to Yuma*) it is sustained right up to and through the climactic gunfight as the lawman's new bride (Grace Kelly) finds herself unwittingly trapped in the crossfire. Also, the film is punctuated with many fine images, from the incidental (for example, a brief close-up of a wagon wheel revolving against the town's façades as Cooper and Kelly make an abortive attempt to leave the community) to the poignant (the camera receding up and away from Cooper's drawn face to show him standing vulnerable and alone in the dust of a deserted main street) to the deliberately melodramatic (Cooper bitterly grinding his marshal's badge in the dirt with his boot before riding away for good at the end of the film).

High Noon also marked the return of Gary Cooper to roles worthy of his talents after a long period of mediocre and unimportant parts. In fact, his performance as Marshal Will Kane won him the year's Oscar. One thing the film could have done without, especially in retrospect, was its

Above left: Gregory Peck as *The Gunfighter* (1950), with Jean Parker, B.G.Norman and Helen Westcott. *Above:* Gary Cooper and Grace Kelly in *High Noon* (1952), with Lon Chaney Jnr a member of the wedding. *Below left and below: Shane* (1953), with Jack Palance gunning down Elisha Cook Jnr, watched by Emile Meyer (in saloon); and, back at the homestead, Jean Arthur, Brandon de Wilde, Van Heflin and Alan Ladd.

highly emotive, artificial and rather trite Tex Ritter theme song – but there is no doubt that it boosted the box-office takings considerably.

High Noon's success provided the real impetus to Western production in the fifties and sixties, aided a year later by another brilliant and influential addition to the genre, George Stevens's *Shane*. Again the theme is a classic (and much-imitated) one: the lone, handsome, mysterious stranger riding into a group of people's lives, sorting out their problems, and then riding out again. The ending of *Shane*, indeed, is one of those rare film sequences which, once seen, are never forgotten, as the farmer's hero-worshipping young son (Brandon de Wilde) watches the stranger ride slowly away in the gathering dusk and then begins to call his name and implore him in vain to come back.

Apart from everything else, *Shane* is an immensely beautiful film, stunningly photographed in colour, whether it is laying stress on the magnificent scenery in which its story is set or the authentic-seeming muddy, shabby township (a saloon, a general store and a few shacks) which has sprung up amidst the pioneer farmers. And it is a film rich in memorable moments: Shane's first appearance in fringed buckskin; his display of dazzling virtuosity with a six-gun; the efforts of Shane and his host (Van Heflin) to uproot a stubborn tree-stump; and – perhaps most vivid of all because of its shock-effect after watching countless cowboys die gentle and totally unrealistic deaths in countless Westerns – the sight of Elisha Cook Jnr's pathetic homesteader slamming back-

Top left: Richard Widmark, Spencer Tracy and Robert Wagner in *Broken Lance* (1954), Edward Dmytryk's study of racial prejudice adapted from the non-Western *House of Strangers*. *Centre left:* Rod Steiger flouting convention by taking an Indian wife (Sarita Montiel) in Sam Fuller's *Run of the Arrow* (1957). *Left and right: The Searchers* (1956), John Ford's haunting story of the hunt by two men (John Wayne and Jeffrey Hunter) for a girl kidnapped by Comanches.

wards through the mud after being shot dead with sadistic relish by cadaverous Jack Palance.

If *Shane* has any major flaws, one is certainly the inadequacy of its star, Alan Ladd, who handles the action splendidly but not the histrionics. He is more than compensated for, however, by the playing of Heflin, de Wilde, Palance, Jean Arthur, Emile Meyer and one of John Ford's favourite hands, Ben Johnson, and by Stevens's immaculate direction which copes with violent action and unashamed pathos with equal assurance.

After the initial impact of the masterpieces of 1950, and of *High Noon* and *Shane*, the Westerns of the fifties took off in all directions, and, partly because big-name directors and stars were now willing to try their hand at the occasional Western, refreshingly ignored any tendency towards specific trends, although certain themes did recur.

Naturally, after *Broken Arrow*'s success, racial themes were tackled from time to time: William Wellman's *Across the Wide Missouri* (1951), which starred Clark Gable, might have had more impact if it had not suffered the fate of its more famous contemporary film, John Huston's *The Red Badge of Courage*, in being mutilated before reaching the screen; *Apache*, an extremely sympathetic portrait of an Indian (played by Burt Lancaster) directed by Robert Aldrich in 1954, was better received; and *Broken Lance*, Edward Dmytryk's film of the same year which dealt with the prejudice (as exuded by a sneering Richard Widmark) against the Indian wife of a white landowner (Spencer Tracy), remains an underrated Western.

The most intriguing and most deeply felt of the post-*Broken Arrow* Indian problem films of the fifties was probably *Run of the Arrow* (1957), a violent and uncompromising movie by the controversial and over-revered Samuel Fuller which credits the Indian with a valid culture and a serious point of view. One of the strengths of Fuller's film is the performance of Rod Steiger as a deserter from the defeated Confederates who marries a Sioux and temporarily embraces the Indian way of life. Another is its honest and unsentimental conclusion, in which Steiger rides away with his Indian wife, unable to accept fully the habits of her people (particularly their innate savagery – he has just seen them skin a white man alive).

John Ford also gave some serious thought, though more remotely, to the white man's irrational hate for the Indian, in his first Western for six years, *The Searchers* (1956). However, although the film's broad theme is of the ten-year search by two men (John Wayne and Jeffrey Hunter) for a girl (Natalie Wood) kidnapped by Comanches, and the Indians are portrayed with dignity and honesty, it is really about Ethan, the character played (quite superbly) by Wayne. He is a loner, a tragic figure displaced by the Civil War and unable to settle down, as he would wish, in a regular family – and over-compensating by his stubbornness in pursuing the abducted girl.

The Searchers is one of Ford's most haunting and melancholic films, and, as always, certain words, sequences, images stay in the mind: Ethan's catchphrase, 'That'll be the day!'; practical Vera Miles giving Jeffrey Hunter an overdue

bath; the opening and closing shots of John Wayne and Monument Valley fittingly framed together through a deeply shadowed cabin doorway.

Other themes recurred during the boom years of the fifties, from the frivolous to the deeply earnest. There was a short vogue for the musical Western (*Annie Get Your Gun, Calamity Jane, Seven Brides for Seven Brothers, Oklahoma!* and the dreadful Western pastiche with Guy Mitchell, *Red Garters*, were all made within the space of five years), and an even shorter one for Westerns with female stars (Fritz Lang's *Rancho Notorious* of 1952 was dominated by Marlene Dietrich, while two years later Joan Crawford gave her characterization of gambling-saloon proprietress Vienna in *Johnny Guitar* all she had got – and was privileged, incidentally, to be on hand in the same film when Sterling Hayden delivered one of the most memorable lines of dialogue to come out of any Western: 'I never shake hands with a left-handed gun!').

The themes which made most impact, however, were those which developed in the work of such strongly individualistic directors as Anthony Mann and Budd Boetticher. Both favoured violent situations and disenchanted heroes stubbornly pursuing some private mission of redemption or revenge (in Mann's films they were usually played by James Stewart, in Boetticher's by Randolph Scott) and both savoured to the full the quirks and neuroses of their villains.

Mann's cycle began in 1950 with *Winchester '73*, continued up to 1958 (his pallid remake of *Cimarron* in 1960 hardly counts here) with *Man of the West*, and included *Bend of the River* (*Where the River Bends* in Britain), *The Naked Spur, The Far Country, The Man from Laramie, The Last Frontier* and *The Tin Star* – a remarkable body of work. *The Man from Laramie*, best known because of the Frankie Laine theme song which accompanied it, is notable for (among other things) Alex Nicol's extraordinary projection of sadism, an element which dominated the best of Mann's movies, *Man of the West*. This starred Gary Cooper instead of Stewart, and its highly charged story of the conflict between two one-time partnered outlaws, one

now reformed, carries strong undertones of sex and violence, the one motivated by the presence of Julie London, the other taken care of by Lee J. Cobb's particularly repulsive villain.

Boetticher's most successful films – those made with Randolph Scott – are basically traditional action Westerns with some added ingredients. Usually they have Scott as a hero of the 'a man's gotta do what a man's gotta do' variety, out to avenge the murder of his wife or a friend, and often the villains, neurotic and cold-blooded, come across as the more interesting characters: Lee Marvin in *Seven Men From Now*, felled conclusively like a pierced bull in the final shoot-out; Henry Silva, bored, icy, half-breed killer in *The Tall T*; Richard Boone, bitterly aware of his own degradation, also in *The Tall T*; and James Best, shrill, whining, tantrum-throwing young punk in *Ride Lonesome*.

Boetticher's taut, economical direction, Burt Kennedy's immortal dialogue ('There are some things a man just can't ride around'), Scott's no-nonsense acting, and the rich gallery of supporting

Far left: Fernando Lamas, Howard Keel and Ann Blyth in Mervyn LeRoy's forgettable remake of *Rose Marie* (1954). *Above left:* Joan Crawford, Ernest Borgnine, Ben Cooper, Royal Dano and Scott Brady in Nicholas Ray's *Johnny Guitar* (1954). *Left and above:* The emergence of Anthony Mann: Arthur O'Connell, Jack Lord, Royal Dano, Gary Cooper and Julie London in *Man of the West* (1958); Millard Mitchell, Robert Ryan, Janet Leigh, Ralph Meeker and James Stewart in *The Naked Spur* (1953).

players, have made this group of films (*Decision at Sundown*, *Buchanan Rides Alone* and *Comanche Station* are the others) among the most satisfying smaller-scale Westerns of recent years.

The middle fifties saw the production of an astonishing variety of Westerns of high quality. Robert Aldrich followed *Apache* in 1954 with a cheerful, action-packed adventure called *Vera Cruz*, which starred Gary Cooper and Burt Lancaster (sporting a disarming but treacherous grin throughout). Its chief highlight is a display of

sharp-shooting in which Cooper and Lancaster demonstrate the effectiveness of the rifles they are trying to sell to a Latin-American governor (George Macready) by snuffing out the torch flames ranged round the palace balustrade.

In the same year, John Sturges, a director of uneven achievement, made an entirely successful modern Western, *Bad Day at Black Rock*, which pitted Spencer Tracy's one-armed lawman (his one arm proving more than a match for the flailing fists of Ernest Borgnine) against one of Robert Ryan's inimitable villains. This gritty, off-beat Western had many of the qualities missing from Sturges's more traditional but more pretentious *Gunfight at the OK Corral* (1957) – though the latter was a hugely successful film – and his somewhat studio-bound *The Law and Jake Wade* (1958), a vehicle for Robert Taylor and Richard Widmark. *The Magnificent Seven* and *Hour of the Gun* were, however, still to come.

Nicholas Ray, who had also tackled a modern theme, rodeo life, in *The Lusty Men* (1952), fol-

lowed his Joan Crawford picture, *Johnny Guitar*, with *Run for Cover* (1955), a rare excursion Westward by James Cagney (though he made the trip again the following year in Robert Wise's *Tribute to a Bad Man*), and *The True Story of Jesse James* (1957), a decent reworking of the West's most enduring badman legend, with Robert Wagner and Jeffrey Hunter as Jesse and Frank.

Other Westerns of more than passing interest at this period included a 1955 project in which Burt Lancaster directed himself as *The Kentuckian*, a disappointing tale of the early frontier which only really comes alive in the occasional set-piece such as Lancaster's frantic dash across a shallow lake to prevent his enemy from reloading his musket; King Vidor's *Man Without a Star* (1955), a fairly routine cattleman-versus-barbed-wire Western dressed up with some sex interest between Kirk Douglas and Jeanne Crain centering on a bathtub; Jacques Tourneur's *Wichita* (1955), which starred Joel McCrea as Wyatt Earp and showed that the traditional values of the Western had not died away; Frank Sinatra's only serious Western, *Johnny Concho* (1956), in which he played a cowardly bully who is finally reformed; and the excellent but largely ignored Delmer Daves movie, *The Last Wagon*, in which a condemned and unrepentant murderer (Richard Widmark) turns out to be the only man sufficiently competent (and ruthless) to lead a wagon train to its destination, and of course proves his worth in so doing.

Daves made a string of superior Westerns towards the end of the fifties, including *3.10 to Yuma*, and *Cowboy* (1958), an attempt at an authentic reconstruction of a cattle drive, with thick-skinned leader Glenn Ford toughening up tenderfoot Jack Lemmon *en route*.

Far left: The burgeoning of Budd Boetticher, with (*above*) Randolph Scott and William Bishop in *Decision at Sundown* (1957); (*above centre*) Skip Homeier, Henry Silva, Scott and Richard Boone in *The Tall T* (1957); and (*below*) Scott, Pernell Roberts, James Coburn and James Best in *Ride Lonesome* (1959). *Above left:* Spencer Tracy, Robert Ryan, Lee Marvin, Walter Brennan and Dean Jagger in John Sturges's contemporary Western, *Bad Day at Black Rock* (1954). *Above:* James Cagney and Viveca Lindfors in *Run for Cover* (1955). *Below:* Burt Lancaster in *The Kentuckian* (1955), which he also directed.

The fifties came to an end with a flourish of fine Westerns, the most outstanding for one reason or another being *The Left-Handed Gun* (1958) and *Rio Bravo* (1959).

The Left-Handed Gun was Arthur Penn's version of the Billy the Kid story, playing havoc with the truth (apart from anything else William Bonney wasn't left-handed), but for once depicting Billy as what he might have been, a petulant, bewildered teenage hoodlum. In many ways Paul Newman's Billy is a precursor of Warren Beatty's Clyde Barrow in Penn's *Bonnie and Clyde*, sharing

his neuroses, his glory-seeking, his death-wish, and his hunt for a parent-figure. In *The Left-Handed Gun* the substitute father turns out to be, of all people, Sheriff Pat Garrett (John Dehner) which is some indication of the individuality of Penn's extraordinary film.

Perhaps in the end there is more symbolism than the simple Western format can take, but Paul Newman's riveting display of 'Method' as Billy is compensation enough, and there are many minor pleasures, not least the playing of James Best as one of Billy's cronies.

For many, Howard Hawks's *Rio Bravo* is the perfect Western. It has been called 'the apotheosis of pride and professionalism', and certainly there is hardly a romantic gesture in the whole film; it is concerned solely with the mechanics of its good guy versus bad guys situation, and with the behaviour under stress of its protagonists. The survivors in Hawks's philosophy are the ones who conduct themselves with the greatest degree of coolness and discipline.

It is not difficult to appreciate why Hawks has used substantially the *Rio Bravo* plot, with only

Above, from the left: Richard Widmark in Delmer Daves's *The Last Wagon* (1956); John Dehner as Sheriff Pat Garrett and Paul Newman as Billy the Kid in Arthur Penn's *The Left-Handed Gun* (1958); and two scenes from *Rio Bravo* (1959), with John Wayne, Dean Martin, Angie Dickinson and Ricky Nelson. *Below, from the left:* Daves's *Cowboy* (1958), with Glenn Ford braving the longhorns; Robert Mitchum in Hawks's *El Dorado* (1967); and Wayne in *Rio Lobo* (1970).

THE WEST'S
MOST SAVAGE
MAN-CHASE
...FROM HELL
TO TEXAS!

THE HELL BENT KID

STARRING

DON MURRAY · DIANE VARSI
CHILL WILLS · DENNIS HOPPER
CO-STARRING

COLOR by DE LUXE
CINEMASCOPE

PRODUCED BY
ROBERT BUCKNER · HENRY HATHAWAY · ROBERT BUCKNER and WENDELL MAYES
DIRECTED BY
SCREENPLAY BY

minor variations (but with a proportionate decline in effectiveness), in both his subsequent Westerns, *El Dorado* and *Rio Lobo*. It is a fascinatingly simple and immaculate piece of engineering, with just enough embellishment of character to round it off and large helpings of action and suspense.

Sheriff John Wayne (at his most superhuman) takes on the forces of evil (in the shape of a gang of local tyrants) with the aid of two deputies – one a lush (Dean Martin), the other a grizzled, semi-crippled old man (Walter Brennan) – and a cool, deadly juvenile gunman (Ricky Nelson). And he wins because his men, for all their shortcomings,

are the professionals, while the opposition are just arrogant amateurs. This is demonstrated in one inspired sequence which has deservedly become a classic: Dean Martin, drying out and eager to win back his self-respect, enters the saloon in pursuit of a wounded assailant; he spots the man's blood dripping from above into a glass of beer and in one movement turns and fires, his opponent's lifeless body crashing to the floor. The old pro clearly hasn't lost his touch – and, as they say in show-business, follow that!

The indefatigable John Ford came near at least to matching it the same year by remaining incorrigibly sentimental and romantic in his big cavalry epic, *The Horse Soldiers*, a Civil War story which has Union officers John Wayne and William Holden leading a mission behind Confederate lines. It is full of heroic cavalry-on-the-skyline imagery – old hat but unfailingly effective – and for those who require it, it is the perfect antidote to Hawks's doctrine of professionalism.

One of the most successful Westerns of the late fifties was William Wyler's massive epic, *The Big Country*, a film disliked by critics but nevertheless hugely enjoyable. The rest of the film never quite retains the impact of those opening scenes, with Gregory Peck and Carroll Baker, harassed by Chuck Connors's taunting, trick-riding cowboys, racing their buggy across a breathtaking landscape while the sound-track hammers out the epic Western theme tune to end all epic Western theme tunes. But it is one of the few large-scale Westerns to convey successfully the true dimensions of the West.

The Big Country rather overshadowed some of the other Westerns of its year. One of them, indeed, Henry Hathaway's rather unhappily titled *From Hell to Texas* (retitled *Manhunt* in Britain) seems to have vanished without trace almost immediately, yet it is highly regarded by connoisseurs and a revival is long overdue. Another, George Marshall's *The Sheepman*, a beautiful mixture of parody and traditional action, has never received the acclaim it deserves. Glenn Ford's performance as an aggressive sheepfarmer is masterly, and the opening sequences in which he anticipates with perfect timing the opposition his sheep are clearly going to cause in a cattle town by co-opting the biggest local rascal as his aide, picking a fight with the town tough guy, and brow-beating the local shopkeepers, are some of the funniest to be seen in any Western.

Yet another underrated Western of the period is

Left: Henry Hathaway's unsung *From Hell to Texas* (1958) with a curious change of title. *Above:* Edgar Buchanan, Glenn Ford and Shirley MacLaine in George Marshall's *The Sheepman* (1958). *Below:* Wallace Ford and Richard Widmark in Dmytryk's *Warlock* (1959). *Bottom:* Carnage in John Wayne's *The Alamo* (1960).

Edward Dmytryk's *Warlock* (1959), a variation on the classic theme of the professional gunman (Henry Fonda) invited to rid a town of its cancerous elements only to be shunned once law and order has been established and a decent lawman installed. It is a taut, subtle, dignified and literate Western, with fine character interplay from Fonda, Anthony Quinn (as his dangerous sidekick) and Richard Widmark (as an outlaw turned sheriff).

The indestructible John Wayne celebrated the advent of the sixties and his fourth decade of film-making by making his début as a director. The result was *The Alamo*, a big, noisy, spectacular fireworks display, but rather vacuous in its reconstruction of the Americans' historical equivalent of Dunkirk. One of its more memorable moments is the death of Jim Bowie (Richard Widmark), stuck with bayonets in the midst of gunning down the Mexican hordes.

The Alamo is somewhat symptomatic of Western production in the early sixties. There were fewer Westerns of importance, and it was often the more modest productions such as *Ride the High Country* which succeeded while the really big blockbuster epics like *The Alamo*, *How the West Was Won* and *Cheyenne Autumn* faltered to a greater or lesser degree.

The big success of 1960, however, and one of the most popular Westerns of recent times, was a fine and spectacular blockbuster called *The Magnificent Seven*. A direct adaptation of Japanese director Akira Kurosawa's period masterpiece, *The Seven Samurai*, its only concession was to substitute professional gunmen for medieval *samurai* and Mexican peasants for Japanese serfs. Otherwise its plot framework of unemployed mercenaries

being hired to defend a humble village against plundering bandits remained unaltered, and, superficially at least, whole characterizations were transferred from Nippon to Texan, as well as physical characteristics such as Yul Brynner's shaven head.

In the hands of an on-form John Sturges, however, the formula couldn't fail as a Western, and the relatively little-known cast were a particularly happy choice, most of them – Steve McQueen, James Coburn, Charles Bronson, Robert Vaughn, Horst Buchholz, Eli Wallach – achieving speedy stardom. It would be churlish, anyway, to cavil at a film which could come up with an opening sequence as exhilarating as the hazardous hearse-ride taken by Brynner and McQueen up to Boot Hill. Sequels such as *Return of the Seven*, dull and unimaginatively cast, have not repeated the film's success.

Kurosawa has proved a rich source of Western material since *The Magnificent Seven*, his *Rashomon* and *Yojimbo* reappearing in somewhat pallid form as *The Outrage* (1964) and the Italian-made *A Fistful of Dollars* (1967) respectively.

John Ford's sixties Westerns, though not his best work, stand out in a lean period. In *Sergeant Rutledge*, made in 1960, he cast Negro actor Woody Strode as the hero, a coloured cavalry sergeant

Left and below left: Eli Wallach (as the bandit chief), Horst Buchholz, Yul Brynner and Charles Bronson in Sturges's *The Magnificent Seven* (1960). *Below:* James Stewart and Richard Widmark in Ford's *Two Rode Together* (1961).

unjustly accused of rape and murder; a brave theme, but a film marred visually by depicting too much studio and not enough Monument Valley. *Two Rode Together* (1961) was disliked by Ford, who made it with some reluctance, and it shows. However, its stars – James Stewart as a cynical sheriff and Richard Widmark as a cavalry lieutenant, bargaining with Comanches for some kidnapped white children – hold it together, while Mae Marsh puts in a welcome appearance.

The Man Who Shot Liberty Valance (1962) is more like the old Ford, perhaps because of the dominating presence of John Wayne, but sadness and introspection have taken over from optimism and sentimentality. Wayne's bitter struggle against Lee Marvin's singularly evil and unpleasant villain on behalf of law, order and political progress (in the person of James Stewart) is grim and without humour. Ford seems in this film to be mourning the Old West.

Ford's last Western (to date) was one of his biggest and most deeply felt: *Cheyenne Autumn* (1964). It tells of the epic and tragic flight of a tribe of Cheyenne Indians, harassed by cavalry, from their reservation in Oklahoma to their native Yellowstone land 1,800 miles away, and for much of its length it is both moving and visually stunning. Unfortunately, it is seriously marred in two respects, one being the disastrous overplaying of Karl Malden, whose neo-fascist army captain would be more at home in *Stalag 17* than in *Cheyenne Autumn*, and the other being the film's Dodge City interlude, an extraordinary sequence designed as comic relief in which James Stewart and Arthur Kennedy enact an outrageous send-up of all the Earp/Holliday movies. It may be in isolation the funniest – and bawdiest – piece of Western parody ever made, but in the context of one of Ford's more sombre themes, it is an inexplicable miscalculation, practically destroying the mood of the film.

To be fair, the finished film was badly cut before release, undoubtedly distorting Ford's intentions. And in spite of everything, there was sufficient genius left for it to survive as a remarkable movie.

Ford also directed one of the episodes (The Civil War) in the gigantic but ultimately tedious *How the West Was Won* (1964). His brief but redeeming contribution effectively recounted the bloody Battle of Shiloh and its aftermath. The film's other directors were George Marshall and Henry Hathaway, who managed some spectacular set-pieces, but failed utterly to come up with the definitive Western as intended.

Two and a bit more films from John Ford: (*left*) *The Man Who Shot Liberty Valance* (1962), with Edmond O'Brien, John Wayne and James Stewart; (*below*) *Cheyenne Autumn* (1964) with Dolores Del Rio and Carroll Baker; and (*right*) *How the West Was Won* (1964), with Karl Malden, Debbie Reynolds, Agnes Moorehead and Carroll Baker, most of which was directed by George Marshall and Henry Hathaway.

The best Western to come out of the sixties – and arguably the best of all time – was by comparison a modest affair: Sam Peckinpah's *Ride the High Country*, or *Guns in the Afternoon* as it was called in Britain. Peckinpah had already given a hint of his powers the previous year with *The Deadly Companions* (1961), but the beauty and originality of his second film were a revelation. It cast veteran stars Joel McCrea and Randolph Scott as two old-timers striving to make ends meet (one legitimately, the other less scrupulously) in a changing West where they no longer belong. They are clearly past it – McCrea goes into a washroom so that he will not be seen donning spectacles in order to read a letter of contract; they sleep in long combs and pause on a tiring journey to bathe their aching feet in a cold stream. And in the end they defend the old values against the new with pride, dignity, never-forgotten skill with six-guns and, for one of them, the blessed relief of death.

Scott and McCrea are perfect in their roles – sincere, poignant, and self-mocking – in what has swiftly become a classic Western.

Peckinpah followed this in 1965 with a more ambitious affair, *Major Dundee*, which starred Charlton Heston as a Union officer in conflict with a defeated but intensely proud Confederate leader (Richard Harris). It was an interesting but unsatisfactory film, evidently much mutilated and disowned by Peckinpah in its release version. Peckinpah's greatest success, however, *The Wild Bunch*, was yet to come.

Among the more interesting and entertaining Westerns of the early sixties were three which had contemporary settings – John Huston's *The Misfits* (1961), which probed the neuroses of Clark Gable, Montgomery Clift, Eli Wallach and (a fine performance) Marilyn Monroe in a rodeo setting; David Miller's *Lonely are the Brave* (1962), which starred Kirk Douglas as the West's last rebel against encroaching civilization, destined to meet his fate under a lorryload of privies; and Martin Ritt's *Hud* (1963), a generation-gap Western, with son-of-a-bitch Paul Newman poisoning the honest values of his rancher father, Melvyn Douglas.

Otherwise, the output was more or less routine, with the fashion for comedy being endorsed by Sinatra and the clan in *Sergeants Three* (1962) and *Four for Texas* (1963), Lee Marvin and Jane Fonda in *Cat Ballou* (1965), and Henry Fonda and Glenn Ford in Burt Kennedy's cheerful *The Rounders* (1965). The 'psychological' Western found a new intensity in a Yul Brynner vehicle, *Invitation to a Gunfighter* (1964), sentimentality and nostalgia

were milked dry in Andrew V. McLaglen's heart-wringing anti-war Western, *Shenandoah* (1965), and old-fashioned ebullience and straightforward action were taken care of by John Wayne in *McLintock!* (1963) and *The Sons of Katie Elder* (1965). Meanwhile, more hints of the explicit violence to come were being dispensed in such films as *Alvarez Kelly* (1966), with the shooting-off of William Holden's finger, *Nevada Smith* (1966), with Steve McQueen's systematic wounding of Karl Malden, and the brutal Marlon Brando vehicle, *The Appaloosa* (1966) – retitled *Southwest to Sonora* in Britain – complete with Indian wrestling performed over a brace of scorpions.

Brando, in fact, was responsible for the most off-

beat Western of the period, *One-Eyed Jacks* (1961), which he directed and starred in. With Monterey seascapes adding a novel touch, this moody, self-indulgent film had Brando as an ex-convict seeking revenge on his betrayer but behaving as if he needed a good psychiatrist rather than a gunfight.

Inevitably, the Western has changed its character in the past five years or so, with the popularity of the synthetic, amoral, sadistic and gratuitously violent European confections forcing producers to imitate their excesses or find new ways to attract an audience. But basically the polished action Western has survived – laced perhaps with more self-mockery than before, but no less enjoyable for that.

Top left: Joel McCrea, Randolph Scott, Ron Starr and Mariette Hartley in *Ride the High Country* (1962). *Left:* Two scenes from *The Misfits* (1961) with Clark Gable, Eli Wallach, Montgomery Clift and (with Gable) Marilyn Monroe. *Above:* Henry Fonda and Glenn Ford in Burt Kennedy's *The Rounders* (1965). *Below, from the left:* Kirk Douglas in *Lonely are the Brave* (1962); Paul Newman and Melvyn Douglas in Martin Ritt's *Hud* (1963); Steve McQueen in *Nevada Smith* (1966); and Marlon Brando in *The Appaloosa* (1966).

Often, when one begins to feel that there hasn't been a good, straightforward Western at the cinema for a long, long time, one pops up to order. In 1966, it was *The Professionals*, a rousing, large-scale affair by Richard Brooks which used to great effect one of the favourite formulas of recent years – the dangerous mission carried out in foreign territory by tough, hand-picked specialists (the explosives expert, the horse-handler, etc.). Since the cast was also hand-picked – Lancaster, Marvin, Palance, Robert Ryan, Woody Strode, not to mention the delectable Claudia Cardinale – and the slices of action filled the screen frequently enough to cover up the plot's inconsistencies, the film was a deserved popular success.

An ingredient which was beginning to creep into this kind of Western, and which is now part and parcel of films like *Butch Cassidy and the Sundance Kid*, was the wisecrack. Where dialogue used to indulge in cracker-barrel philosophy (and still does if John Wayne is around), it now goes in for witticisms, degenerating sometimes into quite childish exchanges like the one in Burt Kennedy's otherwise splendidly ebullient *The War Wagon* (1967) where heroes Kirk Douglas and John Wayne have just simultaneously shot dead a couple of heavies. 'Mine hit the ground first,' says Douglas. 'Mine was taller,' says Wayne.

Left: Karl Malden and Marlon Brando in the latter's *One-Eyed Jacks* (1961). *Above:* Kirk Douglas in Kennedy's *The War Wagon* (1967). *Right:* James Garner in the Burt Kennedy spoof, *Support Your Local Sheriff* (1968). *Below left and below: The Professionals* (1966), directed by Richard Brooks, with Burt Lancaster, Lee Marvin, Robert Ryan and Woody Strode.

The Scalphunters, made by Sydney Pollack the same year, manages a slightly higher level of humour, first of all in its basic situation of an ignorant fur-trapper (Burt Lancaster) coming to terms with the fact that his Negro ex-slave companion (Ossie Davis) is not only an equal but also better educated, and secondly in such inspired moments as that when over-sexed Shelley Winters resigns herself to abduction by Indians because, after all, they are men.

The humour is much broader in *The Good Guys and the Bad Guys* (1969), a kind of comic *Ride the High Country* with George Kennedy and Robert Mitchum in the Scott and McCrea roles, while the same director, Burt Kennedy's *Support Your Local Sheriff* (1968) is pure parody and, as already noted, one of the funniest of all spoof Westerns. James Garner effectively sends up his own TV characterization of Maverick, claiming to be so unimpressed by the so-called Wild West that he plans to emigrate to Australia where the real pioneers are! And in one hilarious sight-gag in which he renders the villain completely impotent by sticking his finger up the man's gun-barrel, every six-gun cliché in the history of the Western is sent flying.

The combination of action and patter reached its irresistible peak in 1969 with George Roy Hill's *Butch Cassidy and the Sundance Kid*, the runaway success of recent years and on its level one of the most entertaining Westerns ever made. Surprisingly, though the characters and dialogue are essentially modern and played for laughs, the film gives a remarkably accurate account of the exploits of these two real-life outlaws, going so far as to ensure that their real names are mentioned (Robert Leroy Parker and Harry Longbaugh) and that Butch refrains from killing anyone until very late in his career (as was the case), and even over-stressing such biographical details as Butch's craze for bicycles. There is also every reason to believe that the real Butch and Sundance were as high-spirited and charming as the superlative performances of Paul Newman and Robert Redford indicate.

On a slightly more serious level, the film does pause long enough to note with a sad smile that these men are the last of the legendary West and that, for all their misdeeds, with their demise all our lives are perhaps a little poorer – a sentiment beautifully conveyed in a delightful pre-credits sequence in which Paul Newman, as Butch, enters a new, strongly secured, heavily guarded bank:

'What happened to the old bank, it was so beautiful?' he asks.

Above left: 'Think you used enough dynamite there Butch? . . .' Robert Redford, Paul Newman and (*above*) Katharine Ross in George Roy Hill's *Butch Cassidy and the Sundance Kid* (1969). *Left:* Charlton Heston as *Will Penny* (1967), directed by Tom Gries.

'It kept getting robbed,' says the guard.

'That's a small price to pay for beauty!'

A variation on this theme, the decline of the cowboy as rude civilization marches into the West, is traced with full seriousness in one of the best of the Westerns to emerge in the new decade, William A. Fraker's *Monte Walsh*.

The tough, lonely life of the cattle drover as it really was had already been touched upon in the beautiful and atmospheric opening scenes of Tom Gries's *Will Penny* (1967), with an aching Charlton Heston forced, at the end of an exhausting cattle drive, to take a humble winter job in the bleak and isolated open air. In *Monte Walsh* this idea is developed at greater length, with Lee Marvin and Jack Palance as itinerant, ageing cowhands seeing out the last days of old-style ranching as the big-city combines move in. The rough, communal,

virtually celibate existence of the working cowboy is marvellously conveyed by Fraker, and he makes the lot of these men as they are made redundant and forced perhaps into crime or aimless wandering, genuinely moving.

Not many of the serious Westerns of the late sixties can match the mood and authenticity of *Monte Walsh*, but there have been some excellent examples none the less. *Hombre,* directed by Martin Ritt in 1966, is a Western of the highest quality. With a plot modelled on *Stagecoach*, an excellent performance by Paul Newman, an equally good one as the villain by Richard Boone, and a con-

ventional but well-handled action climax, *Hombre* takes its place as one of the sixties' best traditional Westerns. Of all the sequences which stay in the mind, perhaps the most memorable is that in which Frank Silvera's bandit painfully congratulates the good guys' marksman every time he is hit.

A notch below *Hombre* perhaps, but much underrated all the same, is Robert Mulligan's *The Stalking Moon* (1968), which has Gregory Peck, with Eva Marie Saint and her half-breed son in tow, being relentlessly hunted across hundreds of miles of country by the boy's Apache-father. The Indian is never seen – he just leaves a wake of dead

Far left: Gregory Peck and Eva Marie Saint in Robert Mulligan's *The Stalking Moon* (1968). *Far left above:* Jeanne Moreau and Lee Marvin in *Monte Walsh* (1970). *Above left and below left:* Paul Newman and Martin Balsam in Ritt's *Hombre* (1966). *Above and below:* Robert Redford as the Deputy Sheriff in pursuit of Robert Blake's rebellious Indian in Abraham Polonsky's *Tell Them Willie Boy is Here* (1969).

bodies. It's a beautifully photographed film, with a fine performance from a stern-faced Peck and an outstanding one from Eva Marie Saint.

A reawakening of sympathy for the Indian is apparent in a number of recent Westerns, notably Abraham Polonsky's *Tell Them Willie Boy is Here* (1969), which tells of the tragic pursuit by a white lawman (Robert Redford) of a rebellious Indian (Robert Blake) in 1909 after the latter has (justifiably in tribal law) killed his girlfriend's father. It is a film worth seeing for Robert Redford's performance alone.

More offbeat is Don Siegel's modern Western, *Coogan's Bluff* (1968), a throwback to the urban Westerns of Hart and Douglas Fairbanks, in which Texas lawman Clint Eastwood takes his rugged outdoor methods to the big city ('This isn't the OK Corral, this is New York') in pursuit of a murderer. Wry and perceptive, it manages to be both exciting and mocking at the same time ('Yeah,' says cop Lee J. Cobb with a scornful sigh when Eastwood asserts that he will not give up pursuit of his man, 'a man's gotta do what a man's gotta do'). Another Siegel Western of this period, *Death of a Gunfighter* (which he took over from Robert Totten), depicts the ironic downfall of a tyrannical lawman (Richard Widmark) made dangerously obsolete by the march of progress; rather an overwrought film, but of above-average interest.

Generally speaking, the big, big Western has come a cropper in recent years – J. Lee Thompson's shoddy and banal *Mackenna's Gold* being a prime example – but there have been two shining exceptions: *The Wild Bunch* and *Little Big Man*, both made by men regarded as 'cult' directors, Sam Peckinpah and Arthur Penn.

The Wild Bunch is an extraordinary Ode to Violence, which really does spell out the death of the West. Its outlaw heroes are weary, desperate men who provoke a town massacre, are relentlessly pursued southwards and end up in a fortified village where they stage a second, suicidal bout of carnage. The film has been attacked for its explicit shots of violence, with the camera lingering over slow-motion blood spurts and bullet-torn bodies. Peckinpah claims that this graphic approach to violence is necessary in order to condemn it, which is questionable in view of its awful, choreographic fascination, repulsive or not.

Below: Warren Oates and Ben Johnson go through their final death-throes in Sam Peckinpah's massive, violent *The Wild Bunch* (1968). *Right:* Richard Mulligan as General Custer making his last stand at the Battle of the Little Big Horn in *Little Big Man* (1970).

Certainly it is far more justified here than in some films unfortunately encouraged by its success to use the same kind of special effects – notably the incredibly clumsy and sickening *Soldier Blue* (however much its director Ralph Nelson may try to make high moral claims on its behalf), and English director Michael Winner's *Lawman*, in which the shattering shoulders and bursting heads are purely gratuitous and just as nauseating.

As a portrait of exhausted heroism, however, *The Wild Bunch* is magnificently moving, and once having seen it, no man's cosy vision of the legendary West with its comradeship and noble sacrifice can be quite the same again.

If anything, *Little Big Man* almost revives the myth that *The Wild Bunch* comes close to destroying. Adapted faithfully from Thomas Berger's superb novel, it is a beautiful mixture of nostalgia and satire; it shows also the deepest understanding yet of the American Indian. The film recounts events in the life of a 121-year-old frontiersman, brought up by the Cheyenne Indians, who claims to be the only survivor of Custer's Last Stand – and whether he is telling the truth or a pack of inspired lies doesn't matter since what he is really doing is re-creating the myth of the West.

Dustin Hoffman, stocky, plain and gauche (his 'old-age' make-up, incidentally, is quite amazing), is perfect as a kind of Western Everyman, meeting Wild Bill Hickok in one episode, surviving an Indian massacre in another, almost assassinating General Custer in yet another. And the Indians, affectionately and intelligently presented by Penn, emerge as exactly what they endearingly call themselves, 'The Human Beings'.

It is difficult to imagine how the Western can progress any further after two such definitive additions to the genre, but doubtless it will. And with a gratifying disregard for any significance which these two blockbusters may pretend to, film-makers have seen fit to fill the opening months of the seventies with Westerns both traditional and experimental.

Peckinpah himself has followed *The Wild Bunch* with a new saga, the intriguing and amusing *Ballad of Cable Hogue*, a not entirely successful attempt to create an instant myth symbolizing the innate nobility and courage of the humble – but not always virtuous – pioneer.

The Indian has received further sympathetic treatment in Elliot Silverstein's unjustly ignored *A Man Called Horse*, a sincere film somewhat sensationalized by its graphic depiction of a savage initiation ritual which includes the hanging of

Left: Dustin Hoffman as *Little Big Man* (1970). *Above:* Kirk Douglas in Joseph L. Mankiewicz's *There Was a Crooked Man* (1969). *Below:* John Wayne, one-eyed in Hathaway's *True Grit* (1968), with Glen Campbell and Kim Darby.

Richard Harris by his pectoral muscles – but containing a stunning vision sequence centering on the symbol of Indian survival, a buffalo. A second Richard Harris vehicle, *Man in the Wilderness*, is also splendid to look at, but less accomplished.

Burt Kennedy has tried again – and failed miserably – to repeat the success of *Support Your Local Sheriff* with another spoof Western, *Dirty Dingus Magee*, with Frank Sinatra, George Kennedy and Jack Elam; while Joseph L. Mankiewicz has had better luck with his comedy-drama Western, *There Was a Crooked Man*, which, with an intelligent script and fine support playing from (especially) Hume Cronyn, pits Kirk Douglas's bespectacled convict against Henry Fonda's respectable prison governor.

For every conventional Western now there is a curiosity to match it. Prolific traditionalists such as Kennedy and McLaglen have plugged along blithely with *The Deserter* and *Hannie Caulder* (Kennedy), *One More Train to Rob* and *Something Big* (McLaglen), disdaining such hit-or-miss oddities as *The McMasters . . .*, with its Negro hero (Brock Peters); the not inconsiderable *Valdez is Coming*, with its Mexican hero (Burt Lancaster); *Zachariah*, the 'first electric Western'; *A Gunfight*, with its double-ended bull-ring showdown between Kirk Douglas and Johnny Cash; the austere, ambiguous *The Shooting* (actually made in 1966); Peter Fonda's introspective *The Hired Hand*; another attempt at the Earp legend, *Doc*, with intentionally ugly heroes (Stacy Keach

and Harris Yulin); and the beautiful, melancholic *McCabe and Mrs Miller*, directed by Robert Altman. Meanwhile, violence has continued to flourish, notably in Robert Parrish's *A Town Called Bastard* and Don Medford's entirely repellent *The Hunting Party*. And for sheer large-scale pretension, Blake Edwards's *Wild Rovers*, with William Holden and Ryan O'Neal, has no recent rivals.

Above all this, however, John Wayne (apparently, with most of his contemporaries dead or retired, out to disprove the concept of mortality) paused after Hathaway's *True Grit* only long enough to collect his Oscar and make a political speech or two before hitting the trail once again in McLaglen's *Chisum*, Hawks's *Rio Lobo*,

George Sherman's *Big Jake* and Mark Rydell's *The Cowboys*. Wayne went on to make five more films before his final appearance, in *The Shootist* (1976), directed by Don Siegel.

If that isn't reassurance enough that the Western still has a few saddle-hours to go, then nothing is.

Below: The Lincoln County range wars as depicted in Andrew V. McLaglen's *Chisum* (1970), yet another variation on the life of William Bonney, with John Wayne as the Kid's mentor and friend.

The STARS

The Western's greatest stars – those who have made major Westerns and either worked exclusively in the genre or made their biggest contribution to the cinema in the Western's broad confines – can be counted on two hands: Anderson, Hart, Mix, Cooper, Wayne, Stewart, Scott, McCrea. But they are only the cream of an endless list of names, some familiar to European audiences, others less so, which have given the Western its special magic and durability: Buck Jones, Ken Maynard, Hoot Gibson, Tim McCoy, William Boyd, George O'Brien, Fred Thomson, Harry Carey, Richard Dix, Johnny Mack Brown, (and though purists may object) Gene Autry, Roy Rogers, *et al.* While to these must be added the numerous stars since the late thirties who have achieved fame in many roles but who have regularly embraced the Western with notable success: Kirk Douglas, Henry Fonda, Glenn Ford, James Garner, Charlton Heston, William Holden, Alan Ladd, Burt Lancaster, Lee Marvin, Robert Mitchum, Paul Newman, Gregory Peck, Robert Ryan, Robert Taylor, Richard Widmark. . . .

All have their place in the history of the Western film and all have their following – but not all, alas, can be fitted into these pages. Here are included only the major stars of the Western, and the more

Left: William S. Hart and Bert Sprotte in Lambert Hillyer's *O'Malley of the Mounted* (1921). *Above:* Randolph Scott in *Abilene Town* (1946).

familiar or original of the series stars. The big-name occasional Westerners such as Fonda, Marvin, Lancaster and Peck have received their due in other volumes, besides getting honourable mention where appropriate in the previous chapter – while the absence of less familiar, more transient minor stars such as Jack Hoxie, Leo Maloney and 'Lash' La Rue will perhaps not be regretted by too many. If, as is inevitable, anyone's special favourite is missing (Rod Cameron? Audie Murphy?), he may well appear as a stalwart later in the book – if not, well, maybe an apology is not enough.

The 'daddy' of all the Western stars – perhaps of the whole Hollywood star system – was **G.M. Anderson**, better known as Broncho Billy. What is more, he outlasted many of his successors, dying as recently as 1971 at the age of eighty-eight.

The image he projected on the screen – the plain, tough, stocky, shy, basically decent frontiersman given to reformation and self-sacrifice – was far removed from the handsome, dashing, romantic hero subsequently favoured by most Western stars, but his was the first screen character which could be identified by the public and they took to it readily.

Anderson was born in 1883 in Pine Bluff, Arkansas. His real name was Max Aronson, which he changed to Gilbert M. Aronson when he started an unsuccessful stage career, changed again to Max Anderson, and finally adjusted to G.M. Anderson when he was becoming established in films.

He began his film career with Edison in 1902 in Edwin S. Porter's *The Messenger Boy's Mistake*, and the following year Porter cast him in *The Great Train Robbery* on the false assumption (conveyed by Anderson himself) that he could ride. In fact, he was thrown on the first day and his appearances in the film were restricted to the train scenes. However, the success of *The Great Train Robbery* convinced Anderson that films were the right business to be in and for a while he worked for such companies as Vitagraph and Selig as actor, director and general assistant. He also learned to ride.

In 1907, finding Selig indifferent to his work, he formed with an old friend, George K. Spoor, a company known as Essanay (derived from their initials, S and A) which later became one of the most distinguished of the early movie studios, promoting the work of Chaplin, Francis X. Bushman and Gloria Swanson, among others. A year later, he took the company to Niles, in California, and there he conceived the idea of a cowboy hero, whom he called 'Broncho Billy', a name filched from stories by Peter B. Kyne.

What he had not conceived was that the star he was creating was to be himself. But California at that time was poorly stocked with actors, and in desperation he took the part himself. The film was called *Broncho Billy and the Baby* and was an immediate success (some sources give the first Broncho Billy film as *The Bandit Makes Good*, which one suspects may be an alternative title for the same film). The public lapped up Anderson's heroic characterization of a good-badman who aids a stricken child and is reformed by love, and so both the name and the characterization (with many variations) stuck, developing into a light industry which produced one- and two-reelers (ten to twenty minutes long) incessantly for the next seven years.

The 400 or more short Westerns which starred Broncho Billy made Anderson a rich man and a national hero, the first idol of the movies. The relative few which survive today, such as *Broncho Billy's Christmas Dinner* and *Broncho Billy's Oath*, reveal why they were so popular – the Billy character had genuine charm, was basically realistic, and could supply sentimentality and action in equal doses.

In 1915, Anderson attempted to make features, but William S. Hart and others had already cornered this market and Billy bowed out. In the early twenties he directed a few Stan Laurel comedies for Metro, but quarrelled with Louis B.

Far left: Broncho Billy Anderson.
*Far left below: Broncho Billy's
Narrow Escape* (1915). *Below
left:* An unidentified Broncho
Billy adventure circa 1912. *Left:*
Tom Mix in *Rustler's Round-up*
(1933), with a youthful Noah
Beery Jnr. *Below:* William Hart in
Three Word Brand (1921).

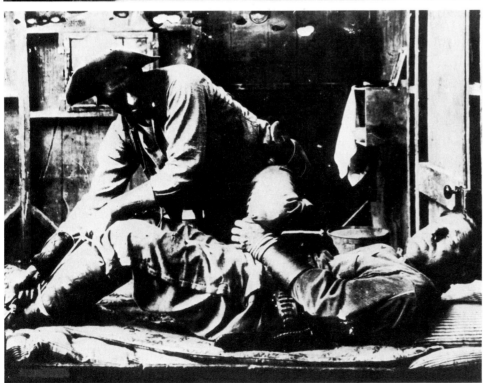

95

Mayer and retired permanently. In the late forties the forgotten Anderson was rediscovered, and in 1958 was awarded a special Oscar for his pioneer work in films. And in 1965 he made his last screen appearance, seated in a saloon in *The Bounty Killer*.

Thus, when his death finally occurred in January 1971, he had received his just acknowledgment for his contribution to cinema history.

William S. Hart ('S' for Surrey) is arguably the greatest of all the Western stars. He never compromised his ideals of always presenting the truth of the West, he devoted himself as actor, writer and director almost exclusively to the genre, and in a career which lasted only eleven years he exerted more influence on the Western's development than any film-maker bar John Ford.

Hart was born in Newburgh, New York, in 1870, but was brought up in South Dakota among the Sioux Indians, and worked as a cowboy in Kansas,

never losing his love for the West. He came to films late in a distinguished stage career, which included both Shakespeare and Western dramas. He was disturbed by the inaccuracy of the Western films he had seen, and in 1914 he persuaded an old buddy, Thomas H. Ince, who had become a film studio boss, to cast him in Westerns.

Ince reluctantly agreed, and after a couple of parts as villains in two-reelers, Hart starred in *The Bargain*, a feature written by himself and C. Gardner Sullivan with Reginald Barker directing. This fortuitous and formidable combination of talents unexpectedly rang the bell first time and while Hart began a fresh rise to fame in his new career, the shrewd Ince began shamelessly to exploit him. So bitter did relations between the two men become at one point that Hart 'retired' his pinto pony 'Fritz' (the movies' first 'personality' horse) from films from which Ince stood to make a profit.

Ince, however, for all his deception, gave Hart his creative head, and with a mixed output of shorts and features Hart rapidly came to dominate the genre under the Triangle banner, toppling Broncho Billy Anderson from his throne as top cowboy star. During this period Hart developed the solemn-faced characterization with which he is indelibly associated, the grim good-badman who achieves redemption by performing noble deeds, usually through the inspiration of a woman's pure love. *Hell's Hinges* (described in the previous chapter) and *The Aryan* were outstanding examples of his Triangle work.

Eventually he fell out conclusively with Ince and joined the Artcraft company, scoring in 1917 and 1918 with *The Narrow Trail* and *Blue Blazes Rawden*. He continued to make high-calibre Westerns right up to 1922, *Branding Broadway*, *The Toll Gate*, *The Testing Block* and *Travellin' On* among them. But by 1920 his popularity had begun to decline. The public had grown tired of the seriousness and obsessive accuracy of his films, while he himself had slowed the pace and increased the sentimental content to a maudlin degree.

Nevertheless, he stubbornly refused to give in to pressures to 'streamline' his films in the Mix style, and disillusioned with the whole business, he cocked a large snook at the industry with his austere but splendid *Tumbleweeds* and retired to his ranch. There he wrote Western books and an autobiography, and gave advice to the industry from time to time. He died in 1946.

Hart has been described as 'the first real figure established by the cinema', and in spite of his faults (his sentimentality and his insistence on playing romantic leads when past fifty years of age – a role he carried over into his personal life) and his lapses (such as the disastrous *Singer Jim McKee*) he retained his integrity and his image of restraint and nobility throughout his dazzling career.

After Hart and Ford, **Tom Mix** was undoubtedly the biggest single influence on the Western in its formative years. Where Hart had instilled realism into the Western and Ford was to provide its poetry, Mix's greatest contribution to the genre was show-manship. He turned the Western into an entertain-ment industry, created many of the traditions of the action Western, and achieved a popularity and box-office value equalled by no other star.

Mix was also one of the few Western stars who could claim to have lived up to his heroic screen image in real life – although his birth (in 1880) occurred in Clearfield County, Pennsylvania, and

Left: Tom Mix. *Top:* William Hart doubly exposed for his dual role in *Three Word Brand* (1921). *Above:* Hart as *Truthful Tulliver* (1917).

not, as is often romantically misreported, in an El Paso log cabin. He saw army action in the Spanish-American War, in the Philippine Insurrection and in the Boxer Rebellion in Peking; he broke horses for the British Army in the Boer War, punched cows in Texas, Oklahoma and Kansas, and sur-vived a firing squad sentence in Mexico. He even served as Texas Ranger, sheriff and deputy US marshal, emulating his later screen escapades by capturing a pair of cattle-rustlers single-handed.

In 1910, after he had joined the Miller Brothers 101 Ranch, a Wild West Show, and become a rodeo champion, he was invited by Selig to handle live-stock for some cowboy documentaries (*Ranch Life in the Great Southwest* was the first), protecting the actors from troublesome animals. This led to doubling and stunting and he inevitably drifted into acting.

Right: Tom Mix in a studio pose to promote *The Canyon of Light* (1926). *Below:* Mix with Patsy Ruth Miller in *The Fighting Streak* (1922).

Mix's first years as a leading player were a hard apprenticeship, and in the seventy short Westerns he made for Selig he achieved only a moderate impact. His stunt-riding was impressive, and one or two titles like *Chip of the Flying U* revealed his potential, but mostly the films were artless and dull.

But the schooling paid off. In 1917 Mix joined Fox and started making fast-action features, with strong production values, skilled direction, and well-chosen locations, and he instantly became a star. By 1920 he had taken over Hart's mantle as the top Western star, and by 1925 – having made Fox's fortune – he was getting the full, lavish Hollywood star treatment, including his own pro-duction unit, a private bungalow and $17,000 per week.

Mix's sixty-odd films for Fox, which included classics such as *Just Tony*, *The Lone Star Ranger*, *The Rainbow Trail*, *The Great K and A Train Robbery* and *Sky High*, were fast, cheerful, high-spirited and streamlined, making no attempt to re-create the real West. In them, Mix rarely used a double, which added to their excitement but took its toll of his physical well-being in later years.

The character developed by Mix on the screen set the pattern for all the horse-opera heroes of the next thirty years until Bill Elliott briefly reverted to the austere Hart image in the early fifties. He didn't drink, swear, treat women disrespectfully or engage in unnecessary violence; and he refrained from killing his foes, rarely even wounding them unless forced to do so. He preferred to capture them with a knock-out punch or fancy ropework. Mix himself summed up the formula thus: 'I ride into a place owning my own horse, saddle and bridle. It isn't my quarrel, but I get into trouble doing the right thing for somebody else. When it's all ironed out I never get any money reward. I may be made the foreman of the ranch, and I get the girl, but there is never a fervid love scene.'

Wholesome stuff – perfectly fit for kids and maiden aunts to watch, as it was intended to be.

Mix was always immaculately dressed in his movies, in an idealized Western costume which was later copied by such stars as Gene Autry and Roy Rogers. He also, because his hands were tender, wore gloves – a gross inaccuracy but one picked up and imitated by many subsequent stars, such was the influence wielded by Mix.

Mix left Fox in 1928 and made a few pictures for FBO (later RKO Radio), and then 'retired' with the coming of sound. He was lured back into the business by Universal, who starred him in the

Above: Gary Cooper and Loretta Young in *Along Came Jones* (1945). *Above right:* Gary Cooper in a Zane Grey adaptation, *Nevada* (1927). *Right:* Cooper as Wild Bill Hickok in *The Plainsman* (1936).

original *Destry Rides Again* and *My Pal the King* – but Mix never took to sound, partly because of poor speech and partly because of physical decline after years of injurious stuntwork. He bowed out in 1934 with a dismal serial called *The Miracle Rider* and afterwards devoted himself to Wild West Show appearances.

In 1940, Mix was killed in a car accident, on the site of which a statue of a riderless pony now stands. In a fabulous career he had become the idol of millions of youngsters, had put such performers as Buck Jones, John Wayne and George O'Brien on the road to stardom, and had created in the Western genre traditions which are still instinctively followed by the newest of film-makers.

Although he made many non-Westerns, **Gary Cooper** is best remembered as one of the great Western stars. With his slow drawl, tall, lean physique, air of innocent integrity and honest determination he became Hollywood's embodiment of the ideal American male. He was also one of the most perfectly natural actors the cinema has produced, with a magnetic screen presence which kept him in the top line for thirty-five years. Colleagues admired him, at least one (Robert Preston) reckoned he was 'the finest motion picture actor I ever worked with', and producer Arthur P. Jacobs called him 'the greatest film star there has ever been – and that includes Gable'.

For many, Cooper was the Westerner *par excellence* – cool, taciturn, courageous and just; skilled with a gun but slow to use it; gentlemanly, rugged and shy, appealing to men as much as to women. This image reached its culmination in *High Noon* with his characterization of Marshal Will Kane, the lawman standing alone against the forces of

Above: Gary Cooper gets rough in *Along Came Jones*.
Above right: Cooper with Maria Schell on the set of
Delmer Daves's *The Hanging Tree* (1959). *Far right:*
James Stewart with a sympathetic Maureen O'Hara
in McLaglen's *The Rare Breed* (1966).

evil, the prototype for countless Western heroes
ever since.

Cooper was born in 1901, in Helena, Montana
and christened Frank James. He was educated
partly in Britain, partly in the States, and in his
late teens, after a bad car accident, he spent some
time on his father's ranch, learning to ride and
absorbing the cowboy life. After trying his hand as
a cartoonist, he became a film extra in 1924, mainly
appearing in quickie Westerns. Then in 1926 he
landed a decent part alongside Ronald Colman and
Vilma Banky in *The Winning of Barbara Worth*
and made a big enough impression to be offered a
long, fat contract by Paramount. It didn't take him
long to captivate cinema audiences with his
appearance in *Wings* (William Wellman's superb
air force epic) and *The Virginian* (the film in which

he first became associated with 'Yep-nope' dialogue), and by the time he had made *The Westerner* and *Northwest Mounted Police* in 1940 he was Hollywood's highest-paid actor at $500,000 a year.

If the Western came to rely on Cooper, he in return could certainly thank the Western for rescuing him from his periodic bad patches. He made four successful ones in the early fifties, *Distant Drums*, *Springfield Rifle*, *High Noon* and *Vera Cruz*, after a run of undistinguished films; and again at the end of the decade, *Man of the West* and *The Hanging Tree* put his more domestic movies such as *Ten North Frederick* in their place.

'Coop' died of cancer in 1961, shortly after receiving his third Academy Award, a special Oscar 'for his many memorable screen performances and for the international recognition he, as an individual,

has gained for the film industry'. They might have added that out of doors no other actor cut a finer figure. He was the Westerner's Westerner.

Cooper's closest friend and associate was **James Stewart**, whose film career has been far more varied but who qualifies as one of the Western's most distinctive stars by dint of many fine appearances in the genre since 1950. His only excursions out West before then had been in the Nelson Eddy/ Jeanette MacDonald musical *Rose Marie* in 1936 (on the wrong side of the law) and the spoof remake of Tom Mix's first talkie, *Destry Rides Again* (1939), as the diffident, gunshy sheriff who prefers words to bullets.

He was born in Indiana, Pennsylvania, in 1908, and started acting at Princeton University. He went to New York in 1932 with fellow-actor Henry Fonda and got a few small parts in plays, and then in 1935 he began his film career with MGM. In his early film years, he developed the characteristic Stewart mannerisms (the stammering drawl, the bewildered look) which have occasionally slipped over into self-parody, and he established his image of the charming, gauche, boy-next-door in several comedies and sentimental dramas. He achieved his best performances in *Mr Smith Goes to Washington* (1939) as the fumbling innocent fighting corruption, and *The Philadelphia Story* (1940), for which he won a Best Actor Oscar.

The transformation came with his two 1950 Westerns, *Winchester '73*, directed by Anthony Mann, and *Broken Arrow*, Delmer Daves's key movie about the Apaches. Both were immensely successful and persuaded him to do two important things: make more Westerns – and go freelance, working for a percentage of gross profits rather than salary. Stewart was the first modern star to make a percentage deal (it had been tried in the silent days) and the scheme's success led to numerous other stars following suit.

Winchester '73 was the beginning of a fruitful association between Stewart and Anthony Mann. Mann specialized in taut, violent, realistic Westerns, and Stewart was frequently the stumbling, brutalized, bewildered, reluctant hero, pursuing some personal mission with grim determination. Together they made *Bend of the River*, *The Naked Spur*, *The Far Country* and *The Man From Laramie*, a remarkable group of films.

Later, he joined John Ford for *Two Rode Together* and, more notably, *The Man Who Shot Liberty Valance*, in which he played a peace-seeking lawyer in a frontier town unable to cope with the West's final manifestations of lawlessness and violence (in the person of Lee Marvin) – a serious version of his Destry role. He also performed hilariously in the comedy sequence of Ford's *Cheyenne Autumn* as Wyatt Earp, delivering the bawdiest punch-line to come out of any Western.

In latter years Stewart has shown no signs of losing interest in the Western, completing three for Andrew V. McLaglen – the emotional but dignified *Shenandoah*, *The Rare Breed* and *Bandolero!* – and joining his old colleague Henry Fonda for *Firecreek* and *The Cheyenne Social Club*, and appearing in *The Shootist*. He embraced the Western relatively late in his career, but did so wholeheartedly and has earned a special place in the history of the genre.

Three decades in the career of James Stewart – impersonating a hangman (*above*) in McLaglen's *Bandolero!* (1968); with Marlene Dietrich (*below*) in *Destry Rides Again* (1939) and (*right*) as *The Man from Laramie* (1955).

Perhaps **John Wayne** (1907–79) will prove to be the greatest Western star of them all. He was certainly the longest enduring (more than forty years at the top), the most successful, the toughest, and the most outspoken.

Wayne's image is one of two-fisted integrity. Boosted by a powerful screen presence, his characters are always larger than life – tough, virile, hard-living and proudly professional; but also sentimental, chivalrous, big-hearted and humorous. He is man and superman. Wayne himself put it more modestly: 'I . . . just sell sincerity. And I've been selling the hell out of it ever since I got going.'

Wayne's real name was Marion Michael Morrison, and he was born in Winterset, Iowa, in 1907. He got his nickname, 'Duke', from a pet dog he had as a youngster. He was brought up in California and attended the University of Southern California on a football scholarship. He was a star player and performed alongside Ward Bond, with whom he teamed up again many times in movies.

Wayne began as a prop man at Fox, working regularly with John Ford, who used him for bit

Above and below: John Wayne in *The Big Stampede* (1932), with Mae Madison.

parts in such films as *Hangman's House* and *Salute* (1929), a football picture. Their early friendship remained constant throughout both their careers. It was Ford who recommended Wayne to Raoul Walsh for *The Big Trail* (1930) in which he landed his first big starring role – and his last for nearly ten years. It was a major production, but not successful, and clearly it was a little early for the Wayne magic to start working.

Throughout the thirties he featured mostly in unremarkable horse operas and serials, with sundry other adventures thrown in, achieving status only as a 'B' player. He even made an abortive attempt to become, long before Ken Maynard and Gene Autry had thought of it, the first singing cowboy – dubbed, not surprisingly.

Then in 1939 John Ford picked him to play the Ringo Kid in *Stagecoach*, and Wayne, quite suddenly, had arrived. The long apprenticeship and the early association with Ford had reaped its reward, and he went on in the forties and fifties to make not only the long string of great Ford Westerns such as *She Wore a Yellow Ribbon*, but also a number of rousing war films like *Back to Bataan* and *The*

Above: Wayne asking Don Douglas for a job in Edwin L. Marin's *Tall in the Saddle* (1944) and (*below*) in trouble in *Haunted Gold* (1933).

Sands of Iwo Jima, Howard Hawks's best Western, *Rio Bravo*, and the immensely successful Irish blarney film (directed by Ford), *The Quiet Man*.

He formed his own production company, Batjac, unwisely tried his hand at direction with *The Alamo*, and maintained his popularity as a star throughout the sixties, prudently allowing touches of parody and self-mockery to creep into what were still often, in spite of increasing corpulence and deepening lines, essentially romantic-heroic roles. Hawks's *El Dorado* (1967) played up this element successfully, and in *True Grit* he finally played his age and the character he now looked like (enhanced by an eyepatch) – a tough, tetchy, hard-drinking, mercenary old-timer. Hollywood and the critics responded with a long-service Oscar, and Wayne continued to ride tall in the saddle with such Westerns as *Rio Lobo* and *Rooster Cogburn*.

Wayne possibly more than any other Western star re-created and heightened the mythology of the West – and if at times his loud mouth and extreme political views reflected poorly on the ideal pioneer image, one has only to watch again his crusty cavalry officer in *She Wore a Yellow Ribbon* or his avenging Ethan in *The Searchers* to be reminded of how irresistible the Duke can be on the cinema screen.

Four faces of John Wayne – (*above*) in Raoul Walsh's *The Dark Command* (1940); (*below left*) with James Stewart in *The Man Who Shot Liberty Valance* (1962); (*below*) in *She Wore a Yellow Ribbon* (1949); and (*right*) as *Big Jake* (1971).

108

Like James Stewart, **Joel McCrea** came into Westerns relatively late in his career, but he took readily to the genre and from the mid-forties scarcely made any other kind of movie. Tall, good-looking and oozing dependability, the character he established was amiable, dignified and peace-loving; not unlike Gary Cooper, in fact, though McCrea had none of Cooper's naturalness. His own modest description of the image he presented on the screen was 'placid'. For twenty years, however, he quietly dominated the main-feature Western, rarely hitting the heights of *Shane* or *High Noon* but consistently turning in honest, reliable performances. If he lacked anything, it was ambition.

McCrea was born in Los Angeles in 1905. As a schoolboy, he anticipated his ultimate career by working both on Californian ranches and as an extra in films. After university he went on the stage, but remained a film extra until picked for a decent part in *The Jazz Age* in 1929. Throughout the thirties he became one of Hollywood's reliable leading men, happy to leave the dizzier heights of stardom to actors like Cooper and Cary Grant.

Then in 1938 he made a very successful Western, *Wells Fargo*, and followed it a year later with DeMille's massive *Union Pacific*, the high point of his popular teaming with Barbara Stanwyck. On the strength of these he started getting excellent dramatic parts – in Hitchcock's *Foreign Correspondent* and two by Preston Sturges, *Sullivan's Travels* and *Palm Beach Story* – but finally settled for the great outdoors, appearing annually up to 1959 in such above-average vehicles as *Buffalo Bill*, *The Virginian*, *Ramrod*, *Four Faces West*, *Colorado Territory*, *Stars in My Crown*, *Saddle Tramp*, *Wichita* and *Trooper Hook*. Few Westerners can boast a finer record.

In 1962, McCrea came out of contented retirement to join fellow-veteran Randolph Scott in Peckinpah's memorable *Ride the High Country*, a happy finale to a pleasing career and a nostalgic reminder of the simple virtues and values of the more traditional Western heroes.

The imperturbable Joel McCrea — with Barbara Stanwyck (*below left*) in DeMille's *Union Pacific* (1939); with Ramon Novarro (*right*) in *The Outriders* (1950); and with Barbara Britton and Sonny Tufts (*below*) in Stuart Gilmore's version of *The Virginian* (1946).

Like McCrea, **Randolph Scott** did not become exclusively a Westerner until the mid-forties, but once established he became a Western star of distinction, achieving his best and most interesting roles as his career matured.

Scott was known as the 'Gentleman from Virginia' (he was born there in 1903) and gentlemanliness was indeed the prime quality he brought to his many roles as lawman or lone rider (though he could be tough, laconic and tight-lipped when action was called for). His accent and breeding have often, in fact, been a subject for affectionate humour, both on screen and off. Lee Marvin, unofficial chief raconteur of Randolph Scott anecdotes, recalls seeing him 'sitting there immaculate on the set as his stuntman went by on the burning stagecoach. He didn't even look up. Just went on reading the "Wall Street Journal".'

Scott began his career on the stage in California, sharing the tribulations common to all aspiring actors with his friend Cary Grant. He got his first good film part in *Sky Bride* in 1931 and settled down to a mixture of adventures, romantic dramas and Westerns, but in the late thirties and early forties began to star in large-scale Westerns such as *The Texans*, *Western Union*, *Frontier Marshal* and *The Spoilers*, which made his reputation in the genre. And after a few excursions into war movies, he stayed permanently in the saddle.

Scott's best work was the group of seven movies he made with director Budd Boetticher in the fifties: *Seven Men From Now* (with Marvin), *Decision at Sundown*, *The Tall T*, *Buchanan Rides Alone*, *Ride Lonesome*, *Westbound* and *Comanche Station*. In these he attained a new stature as the lone figure on a mission of vengeance or similar private quest, becoming a tougher, more forceful character, the archetype of the much-parodied 'a man's gotta do what a man's gotta do' image. He finally rounded off this splendid climax to a long career by starring with Joel McCrea in *Ride the High Country*, as described previously.

Lee Marvin tells another story about Scott: 'He's mad keen on golf. So he tries to join the club at Beverly Hills. But they say, "We're very sorry, sir, there are two kinds of people we can't admit, Jews and actors." So Randy says, "I'm not an actor – and I've made twenty-five films to prove it." So they let him in. . . .' In fact, he made many more films to prove that he was a perfectly adequate actor, besides which he had a fine screen presence and will remain one of the most respected of all Western stars.

Randolph Scott, a star in maturity – with Claude Akins (*below left*) in *Comanche Station* (1960); with Manuel Rojas and L.Q.Jones (*right*) in *Buchanan Rides Alone* (1958); and (*below*) in Sam Peckinpah's *Ride the High Country* (1962).

After Tom Mix (and possibly Fred Thomson, immensely popular star of the twenties who died at the end of the silent period and is barely remembered now) **Buck Jones** was the best loved and most idolized of the series Western stars. Yet unlike Mix, to whom he was second-string at Fox in the twenties, he made a successful transition into talkies, achieving a twenty-five-year career which was still progressing strongly when he died tragically in 1942 trying to rescue people trapped in the catastrophic 'Coconut Grove', Boston, night-club fire. He was one of nearly 500 victims.

Jones was born in Vincennes, Indiana, in either 1889 or 1891 (sources differ) and was brought up on a ranch in Oklahoma, where he learned to ride expertly. He tried his hand as a car mechanic and served with the US Army on the Mexican border and in the Philippines before becoming a trick rider in the Miller 101 Ranch Wild West Show. Subsequently he joined the Ringling Brothers Circus and in 1917 became a film extra, stunting and doubling for Hart, Mix, William Farnum and other stars. In 1919 he was given his first leading role in *The Last Straw* and rapidly became a top star at Fox, occasionally making non-Westerns.

Jones's style was a compromise between the gaudy showmanship of Mix and the austere realism of Hart; the films following the exciting Mix format in action and plot, but Jones dressing more soberly and playing with more restraint. He also injected comedy and folksy humour, usually poking the fun at himself rather than at a comic sidekick.

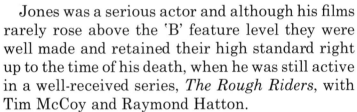

Jones was a serious actor and although his films rarely rose above the 'B' feature level they were well made and retained their high standard right up to the time of his death, when he was still active in a well-received series, *The Rough Riders*, with Tim McCoy and Raymond Hatton.

This page: Buck Jones vehicles of 1934–35 – *Rocky Rhodes* (*above left*); *Stone of Silver Creek* (*above*); and *The Crimson Trail* (*below*) with Ward Bond. *Right:* Harry Carey in 1925.

Another early star who retained some of the Hart characteristics was **Harry Carey**, though his essential seriousness, mature looks and emphasis on plot rather than athletic stunts prevented him from attaining the popularity of Buck Jones and other more flamboyant contemporaries. He was, however, well liked and long-enduring, becoming a character actor in the thirties and making appearances well into the forties in such films as *Duel in the Sun* and *Red River*.

Carey was born in 1878 in New York's Bronx and began his career in films in 1909, working often for D.W.Griffith. Later he became a star primarily of Westerns, the best of them directed by John Ford who, after Carey's death in 1947, dedicated his 1949 remake of *Three Godfathers* to the star's memory. He is remembered mainly for his strong, intelligent portrayals of rugged men engaged in moral rectitude, in such films as *Satan Town* and *The Prairie Pirate*. During the silent period, at least, he was one of the Western's biggest stars.

Harry Carey – (*above*) in *The Texas Trail* (1925), and (*left*) with his sister-in-law Mignenne, in *The Kick Back* (1922). *Right:* Donald Pleasence practising his own brand of sadism on Charlton Heston in *Will Penny* (1967).

One of the most popular and likeable Western stars of the twenties was **Ken Maynard** (1895–1973), flamboyant in the Tom Mix vein and an exceptionally skilled trick rider.

He was born in 1895 in Mission, Texas, had become a champion rodeo rider by 1920, and began in movies by playing Paul Revere in *Janice Meredith* in 1924. For a while he made cheap movies which mainly showed off his riding skill, and then in 1926 he came into his own with a remarkable series of films for First National which were among the best action Westerns ever made and were by 'B' feature standards quite exceptional.

The first of these was called *Senor Daredevil* and was an immediate hit. Of those that followed *The Red Raiders* is the one most quoted as an outstanding example: it was slick, streamlined and made on a large scale, with fast, spectacular action and fluid, imaginative camera-work. Maynard's stunt-riding, in particular, was shot with maximum effect, often in close-up. Maynard himself was at

Ken Maynard — pinned down (*above*) in *The Fiddlin' Buckaroo* (1933); and (*right*) as he appeared in 1929 prior to starring in Harry Joe Brown's *The Wagonmaster. Left and above left: How the West Was Won* (1964) with (at the bar) Richard Widmark.

his prime during this period, dashing, handsome and dazzlingly athletic.

Maynard crossed over into talkies with reasonable success (although ·he was never entirely at ease with dialogue) and continued to make films in considerable quantity right up to 1946. He was the precursor of the singing cowboy, often interrupting the incessant action with scenes in which he himself sang a number or which featured a singing group of cowboys. Gene Autry made his début in one of these films.

Maynard's movies after 1930 never matched his First National spectaculars, but they alone ensure him a place among the great Western stars.

Hoot Gibson (christened Edmund Richard) was another highly popular and long-lasting series star responsible for streamlining the Western and removing it from the real West. Born in Tekamah, Nebraska, in 1892, he was a genuine cowboy,

winning the title 'Champion Cowboy of the World' in 1912 and becoming one of Hollywood's best and most daring stuntmen.

Gibson made numerous quickie Westerns until the twenties, when he embarked on a series of entertaining features and shorts for Universal. His style was to combine comedy and modern story lines, with little action (but enough nevertheless to keep the fans happy) and no violence (he hardly ever wore a gun). Occasionally he starred in a more conventional 'special' such as *The Flaming Frontier*, a version of Custer's Last Stand, but he was best liked for the novelty of such light-hearted affairs as *The Phantom Bullet*, which incorporated a spectacular motor-car stunt.

Thereafter, although he continued to make films until his death from cancer in 1962 (John Ford, for whom he had starred in the early days, used him in *The Horse Soldiers* in 1959), the quality of his pictures declined.

Far left above: Hoot Gibson. *Above left:* Gibson as he appeared in *The Boiling Point* (1932). *Above and above right:* Tim McCoy in *West of Rainbow's End* (1938). *Far left:* Gene Autry and 'Champion' surrealistically posed. *Left:* Autry in Alfred E. Green's *Shooting High* (1940) with Jane Withers. *Right:* Autry and Gail Davis in *On Top of Old Smoky* (1953).

One more name which should be added to the half-dozen or so top Western stars of the twenties is that of **Tim McCoy** (1891–1978), dignified Colonel in the US Army and an authority on Indian lore. Born in 1891 in Saginaw, Michigan, he lived as a young man on a Wyoming ranch next to a Sioux reservation, entering movies by acting as adviser on Cruze's *The Covered Wagon*. Two years later he attracted attention as an actor in a Zane Grey adaptation, *The Thundering Herd*, and was put under contract by MGM for a series of big-budget historical Westerns. These were against the grain, stressing story as well as action and aiming at an adult audience, but they made McCoy a star of some stature.

McCoy was a good actor (when he wasn't overdoing his icy stare) and despite his less immediate appeal survived into the thirties and far beyond, making appearances as far on as 1957 (*Run of the Arrow*) and even 1965 (*Requiem for a Gun-*

fighter). He is most easily remembered by the unusual but distinctive all-black costume which he
took to wearing in the thirties, and which was
imitated by William Boyd in his Hopalong Cassidy
roles.

Whatever one's opinions of the singing cowboys
of the thirties and forties, two of them at least,
Gene Autry and Roy Rogers, became immensely
popular and merit inclusion here as major Western
stars – even though, as one chronicler puts it, their
films are 'more important for their volume and
economic significance than for any artistic worth'.

Gene Autry was the first singing cowboy of any
substance and the dominant Western star for six
highly profitable years, often being listed in Hollywood's top ten box-office favourites. He was also
the first Westerner to use his own name in his
films, a practice followed by Roy Rogers and others,
and the first to take streamlining to its ludicrous
limits in combining traditional Western ingredients (cattle stampedes, fist-fights, gun-duels, etc.)
with modern innovations (aircraft, fast cars, political jamborees, jet-rockets, etc.). None of these
elements did the Western any good (except maybe
financially), but the public lapped them up.

Autry was born in Tioga, Texas, in 1907, and left
school in 1925 to work as a railway telegraph
operator. On the advice of Will Rogers he took up
singing professionally and became a popular radio
vocalist, teaming up with a low-comedy sidekick,
Smiley Burnette, who partnered him in many of his
films. They were signed up by Republic Pictures
and made their début in two Ken Maynard movies,
Mystery Mountain and *In Old Santa Fé*. A serial,
Phantom Empire, followed, but the big breakthrough came in 1935 with *Tumbling Tumbleweeds*, which set the pattern of giving action and
songs an equal share of screen time.

Autry's popularity continued unabated until
1942, when he joined the war and Roy Rogers began
to take over his mantle. After the war he resumed
his career in stronger 'B' features with less vocal
interruption, and went on to consolidate his considerable wealth with radio and television shows
and promotion of the 'Gene Autry Rodeo'.

An interesting element in all Autry's movies was
their Boy Scout morality, which he took to greater
lengths than any comparable Western star. He
rarely kissed his leading ladies, and when he did so
it was usually with bashful reluctance, his horse
'Champion' nudging him into it and the camera
turning away considerately at the moment of impact. He also drew up the widely approved 'Ten

Left: Roy Rogers aiding and abetting Bob Hope's
send-up of the West in *Son of Paleface* (1952).
Above: Rogers with his wife and leading lady,
Dale Evans.

Commandments of the Cowboy', which stressed
fair play, truthfulness, patriotism, respect for
women, parents, animals and old folk, religious
and racial tolerance, cleanliness of thought and
speech, etc. – all thoroughly bland and wholesome,
and suitable for his mainly youthful audience.

For a performer of such average ability and
personality, Autry's rise to stardom must be regarded as phenomenal. One can only suppose that
he hit the right note at the right time.

Autry's only real rival in the sphere of the singing
cowboy was **Roy Rogers**, who was initially
developed by Republic as second-string star to

Autry, but who eventually replaced him in popularity.

Born Leonard Slye in Duck Run, Ohio, in 1912, Rogers was initially a singer under the name Dick Weston, helping to form the famous cowboy singing group 'The Sons of the Pioneers' who were used often by John Ford. He had been shrewd enough to spend a year on a Montana ranch learning to ride and shoot, and his first starring vehicles (after bit parts in Autry movies, among others) from the 1938 *Under Western Stars* onwards had stronger Western elements than Autry's. His sidekick, Gabby Hayes, was an improvement, too, on Smiley Burnette.

Once Rogers had the field to himself, however, he became 'King of the Cowboys' and, backed by much larger budgets, made what amounted to musical extravaganzas. Films like *Idaho* and *The Cowboy and the Senorita* were hardly Westerns at all, in fact, though *Heart of the Golden West* and *Silver Spurs* were a more acceptable combination of song and action. Later, when the novelty of music had worn off, quite brutal action became a prominent part of the Rogers Westerns.

As well as being the most popular series star after Autry's decline, Rogers could claim to be the most immaculate (he and his leading lady – later his second wife – Dale Evans wore extremely ornate cowboy costumes), to own the most famous horse ('Trigger', billed as 'the smartest horse in movies') and to be Hollywood's most commercial actor, coining it from numerous tie-ups with toy and apparel manufacturers. He was not so much a star as a one-man industry.

Like Autry, Rogers successfully exploited television and the rodeo circuit, and (an overt Christian) stressed the morality of his screen image: 'We feel we owe it to the kids who see our pictures to lead homely, wholesome lives.' Of the rivalry between Autry and himself he could afford to take a generous view: 'He has his following, we have ours. There's plenty of room on the prairie.'

Big-name Westerners: (*top left*) Lee Marvin and Burt Lancaster in *The Professionals* (1966); (*centre left*) Robert Mitchum in *The Wonderful Country* (1959); (*left*) Alan Ladd in *Red Mountain* (1952), with Arthur Kennedy, John Ireland and Neville Brand; (*above right*) Kirk Douglas in *The War Wagon* (1967); (*far right*) Glenn Ford and William Holden in *The Man from Colorado* (1948), and Richard Widmark in *Alvarez Kelly* (1966); (*right*) Henry Fonda in *The Ox-Bow Incident* (1943).

The STALWARTS

The names in this chapter are just a selection from the vast 'repertory company' of actors whose dependable presence has given the Western its essential colour, magic, stability and durability. Often it has been they rather than the star who have whetted one's appetite for a film or rescued it from tedium. Often their very familiarity (of face if not of name), their mannerisms and their utter predictability have added the vital ingredient of pleasure to the experience of watching a Western. An item as small as Andy Devine's whine or Jack Elam's wild eye can do the trick as easily as a cameo by John Carradine or a whole performance by Victor McLaglen.

What follows is a far from complete round-up of the better-known minor stars (in some cases not so minor, namely George O'Brien and Johnny Mack Brown), sidekicks, heavies and character actors who have helped to re-create the mythology of the West on the cinema screen. Some have not restricted themselves to Westerns – others have been excluded because Westerns formed only a small part of their output. Again, if your favourite isn't here (L.Q.Jones? Strother Martin?) we can only apologize and plead that the line has to be drawn somewhere.

Left: Robert J. Wilke about to pit his gun against James Coburn's knife in *The Magnificent Seven* (1960). *Above:* Audie Murphy in *Cast a Long Shadow* (1959).

Rodolfo Acosta (1920–74), sometimes called 'Rudy', was one of the most familiar of screen Mexicans, his prominent cheekbones, mean, narrow eyes and supercilious mouth placing him more often than not among the villains – or the Indians. Chihuahua born, he was also one of the few genuine Mexicans in Hollywood movies.

He made some notable Mexican films from 1946 before moving to Hollywood in 1950. He thereafter featured as henchman or hired gun in many memorable Westerns, including *The Proud Ones, One-Eyed Jacks, How the West Was Won, The Sons of Katie Elder* and *Return of the Seven.*

Surly villain, bully and troublemaker is the composite image usually presented by heavy character actor **Claude Akins** (b. 1918), former Broadway actor who has been in films since *From Here to Eternity* (1953). He was at his nastiest in *Rio Bravo* as smooth cattle baron John Russell's loutish brother, baiting lush Dean Martin by tossing a dollar into a spittoon, and cold-bloodedly murdering an unarmed man. And he effectively harassed Randolph Scott in *Comanche Station.*

With his 'big bear' physique, Akins can as easily portray the sad, soft-hearted tough guy, as in *Return of the Seven,* or the comic oaf, as in *The Last Warrior.* Other appearances include *Johnny Concho, How the West Was Won* and *Waterhole No. 3.*

Like his younger compatriot, Rodolfo Acosta, **Pedro Armendariz** (1912–63) was a star of

Mexican films before he made his name in Hollywood, usually portraying a suffering, lugubrious, brutish peasant. In his small number of Western roles he could be cruel, ruthless and corrupt, as in Robert Parrish's *The Wonderful Country*; but he was more often sympathetic, especially in the John Ford films *Fort Apache*, in which he played a loyal sergeant, and *Three Godfathers*, in which he was one of the trio of kindly outlaws who adopt an orphaned baby.

Armendariz committed suicide in 1963 when he learned that he had an incurable cancer.

Warner Baxter (1892–1951) – survivor of the San Francisco earthquake in 1906 – was really an all-round star, one of the biggest of the twenties and thirties when his mature, manly, reliable, executive-type image was in demand. But he merits inclusion here as being the best of the few actors who have portrayed O. Henry's famous character,

Above: Claude Akins (right) in *Comanche Station* (1960). *Below:* Rodolfo Acosta (centre) in *Bandido* (1956). *Right:* Warner Baxter (centre) in *The Return of the Cisco Kid* (1939) with Cesar Romero (left). *Below right:* Pedro Armendariz (with ladle) in *Fort Apache* (1948) with Victor McLaglen, Dick Foran and Jack Pennick.

the Cisco Kid (the others were Cesar Romero, Gilbert Roland and Duncan Renaldo).

Baxter played the part for the first time in the enormously successful *In Old Arizona* (1929) – the first 'outdoor all-talkie' – and earned himself the Oscar for Best Male Actor in only the second year it was awarded. He repeated the role in *The Arizona Kid* (1930), *The Cisco Kid* (1931) and *The Return of the Cisco Kid* (1939), the last of which featured Cesar Romero in a small part.

Other Westerns in which Baxter starred included the third version (out of four) of the classic Indian love story, *Ramona*, in which he portrayed the noble Alessandro opposite Dolores del Rio; DeMille's second remake of *The Squaw Man* as the aristocratic Englishman who goes West; and William Wellman's *The Robin Hood of Eldorado* as the Mexican bandit Joaquin Murietta.

He died in 1951 of bronchial pneumonia after making a string of second features in the forties.

Wallace Beery (1886–1949) was another big star of Baxter's period who gave some of his best performances in Westerns, usually as a heavy. A big, burly, spectacularly ugly man ('my mug has been my fortune'), one-time assistant elephant trainer, musical comedy baritone and female impersonator, Beery came to specialize in soft-hearted bad guys, stretching his lovable-rogue image to the limit in *The Badman of Wyoming* (1940) and *Bad Bascomb* (1946). In the latter he played a ruthless outlaw reformed by sweet Margaret O'Brien.

Beery played down the sentimentality in his more memorable roles, such as Sheriff Pat Garrett in King Vidor's *Billy the Kid* (1930) and Mexican revolutionary Pancho Villa in *Viva Villa!* (1934). His other Westerns included *The Last of the Mohicans* (1920), *The Great Divide* (1925) and *The Pony Express* (1925).

Beery's nephew, **Noah Beery Jnr** (b. 1916), who played opposite him in *Twenty Mule Team* (1940), has settled into more comfortable familiarity in Westerns as the soft-spoken country boy and hero's buddy – supporting Tom Mix, Johnny Mack Brown and Randolph Scott, among others. Apart from *Red River* and one or two other large-scale Westerns, most of his work has been in second features.

Above: Wallace Beery (left) in *Viva Villa!* (1934). *Below:* Noah Beery Jnr in *Red River* (1948). *Above right:* Edgar Buchanan (left) and Lyle Bettger (centre) in *Destry* (1955) with Audie Murphy. *Below right:* Charles Bickford in *The Big Country* (1958) with Carroll Baker, Gregory Peck and Charlton Heston.

Lyle Bettger (b. 1915) is one of those stalwarts whose names probably mean nothing to most average filmgoers but who enjoy instant recognition on the screen. (Henceforth, such regulars as these shall be known as Familiar Faces.)

Bettger began as a leading man in 1946, but is now far better known (and better off) as a blond, blue-eyed villain given to exuding pathological hatred. His credits include *Destry*, *Gunfight at the OK Corral* and *Nevada Smith*.

One of Hollywood's most dependable and versatile light-heavies for nearly forty years, **Charles Bickford** (1889–1967) could as easily play the sincere man of virtue as the unscrupulous villain. His rugged manner and stubborn face suited him perfectly to such roles as the proud but misguided patriarch leading the 'good' side in the range war against Burl Ives in *The Big Country*.

A stage actor for some years, Bickford entered movies in 1929 and appeared regularly in good Westerns, of which *Hell's Heroes*, *The Squaw Man*, *The Plainsman* (he is the one who tries to knife Gary Cooper), *Duel in the Sun*, *Four Faces West* and *Big Deal at Dodge City* stand out.

One of the Western's best-known and most popular character actors was **Ward Bond** (1905–60), who looked particularly at home as the pugnacious but respected cavalry NCO or chief spokesman for the pioneers.

His first part was for John Ford alongside John Wayne in the football picture *Salute*, after which he spent the thirties playing villains opposite Buck Jones, Ken Maynard, Tim McCoy and Wayne. He became stereotyped as a tough bully (e.g. in *The Oklahoma Kid*) before Ford started giving him more interesting and more substantial roles. He had good parts in *Drums Along the Mohawk, My Darling Clementine, Fort Apache* and *Three God-fathers*, and then had his best opportunities in *Wagonmaster*, as leader of the Mormon pioneers, and *The Searchers* as John Wayne's fighting companion.

In 1957 Bond achieved stardom on television as Major Seth Adams, the wagonmaster in the *Wagon Train* series, but died of a heart attack three years later.

There has been no tougher or more formidable Western heavy than **Richard Boone** (b. 1917). He has occasionally depicted hard-bitten nobility, as in his portrayal of General Sam Houston in *The Alamo* or the ageing cavalry officer in *A Thunder of Drums* – but more often his grim, craggy features have led him into villainy.

He was Randolph Scott's intelligent, embittered adversary, smooth as a rattlesnake and twice as treacherous, in *The Tall T*; he wrapped non-conforming farmers in barbed wire in *Man Without a Star*; as mean, sadistic Major Salinas, he persecuted Rory Calhoun in *Way of a Gaucho*; and he gave Paul Newman a rough ride in *Hombre*.

A fine, respected actor and powerful presence, Boone is one of the screen's most efficient scene-stealers.

William Boyd (b. 1898) had been in films with reasonable success for sixteen years, notably as a favourite DeMille actor, before he made his first appearance as Hopalong Cassidy in 1935. The character was such a success that Boyd did little else for the next sixteen years except make Hopalong Cassidy movies – and when he called it a day in 1951 the tally was sixty-six. A TV series subsequently swelled the number even further.

The Cassidy character hit it off in Boyd's interpretation by being mature, thoughtful, soft-spoken, gentlemanly and non-violent – although the films satisfied younger audiences by guaranteeing a thrilling action climax. It was one of the most successful and enduring screen characters ever devised.

Walter Brennan (1894–1974) was the most 'decorated' character actor in American movies, with three Academy Awards for Best Supporting Actor to his name, one of them for his memorable study of Judge Roy Bean (the 'Hanging Judge') in *The Westerner*.

From his beginnings in films in the early twenties, Brennan acted the gamut of Western characterizations, from villainy to comedy, in later years sticking almost exclusively to garrulous, stubbly old-timers. *Law and Order, The Texans, Northwest Passage, Red River, The Far Country* and *The Proud Ones* are among his more notable Westerns, but apart from *The Westerner* he will be best remembered as the lame, grumpy old jail-keeper in *Rio Bravo* and the evil Old Man Clanton in *My Darling Clementine*, obsessively protecting his brood of murderous sons.

Above: Ward Bond in *The Halliday Brand* (1957) with Viveca Lindfors. *Above right:* Richard Boone in *The Alamo* (1960). *Far right above:* William Boyd as Hopalong Cassidy (left) and Andy Clyde (centre) in *Pirates on Horseback* (1941) with Russell Hayden. *Right:* Walter Brennan as Old Man Clanton in *My Darling Clementine* (1946) with Henry Fonda.

Before he made a surprising transition to starring roles, e.g. *Death Wish, Once Upon a Time in the West,* **Charles Bronson** (b. 1922) had a good run as all-purpose Western heavy from the early fifties, mainly – thanks to his Slav appearance – in Indian roles. A good example was his junior chief in *Run of the Arrow.* His best – and most sympathetic – supporting role was as the silent, soft-hearted gunman doted on by Mexican peasant children in *The Magnificent Seven.*

Johnny Mack Brown (1904–79) perhaps more rightfully belongs among the stars, but he was not an innovator, and, apart from one major starring role as Billy the Kid, remained firmly entrenched in 'B' features during his twenty-year film career (not counting a couple of comeback appearances in 1965).

Brown was in fact a better actor than most of his colleagues, having played straight dramatic roles opposite Garbo, Pickford and Joan Crawford in the twenties. He was also sober in appearance, presented a modest, likeable image, and handled his action well; a reliable, popular Westerner.

Above: Charles Bronson in *Villa Rides* (1968) with a hirsute Yul Brynner. *Below:* Johnny Mack Brown in *The Oregon Trail* (1936). *Above right:* Marilyn Monroe in Otto Preminger's *River of No Return* (1954). *Below right:* Dean Martin in *Five Card Stud* (1968).

Edgar Buchanan (1902–79) was the Western's archetypal grizzly-bearded rogue, a dab hand at drunken oldtimers and corrupt officials (judges, mayors, etc.). He squinted and scowled through numerous Westerns, big and small, including

Above: Smiley Burnette in *On Top of Old Smoky* (1953) with Gene Autry. *Left:* Steve McQueen in *Nevada Smith* (1966).

Shane and *Ride the High Country* – but perhaps his finest moments were in *The Sheepman* as the town 'character', the sly, mercenary old-timer tamed by Glenn Ford and allocated the job of feeding him the latest gossip and running his errands.

Smiley Burnette (1911–68) requires no more than a passing mention as Gene Autry's long-serving but tiresome sidekick, the first non-hero to get on to the list of top ten cowboy stars in the forties. He was tubby and wore the statutory funny hat with flattened brim, and his brand of hillbilly low comedy was fairly insufferable.

Rory Calhoun (b. 1922), who started life as Francis Timothy Durgin, began in films in 1944 through a friendship with Alan Ladd after experience in lumber-camps and on ranches. In spite of good looks, a pleasantly wry personality and an easy manner, however, he never quite made top stardom, and none of his Westerns is especially memorable. Yet he had a following, and regular Western fans will recall him in *Way of a Gaucho*, *Powder River*, *River of No Return* and *Apache Territory*.

Another minor star with a decent following was Canadian **Rod Cameron** (*né* Cox in 1912), who doubled for Buck Jones, started as a bit-player in 1939 and helped to fill a large quota of 'B' feature backgrounds before landing his first big role in *Salome, Where She Danced* (1945). Thereafter he worked steadily in small-scale Westerns, occasionally appearing in better-grade movies such as Lesley Selander's *Panhandle* (1947), *The Bounty Killer* and *Requiem for a Gunfighter*.

A stolid, inexpressive player of massive build, considerable height and rock-carved features, Cameron lacked the personality to sustain top-rank stardom, but he has lasted well.

Yakima Canutt (b. 1896) has earned a special honoured place in the history of the Western as one of its most skilled, spectacular and audacious stuntmen and stunt innovators, a stalwart of one kind or another since 1924. In addition to being Hollywood's supreme stuntman, he has also earned respect as silent star, character actor and, latterly, second-unit director (in which capacity he handled the chariot race in the 1959 *Ben Hur*). Some of his best work was in the Indian attack sequence in *Stagecoach*, a vivid demonstration of his real speciality, falls from horses; and in *The Devil Horse* (1932) he was the one who literally fought the horse, dangling by his feet from its neck.

After his brief spell as an action star, Canutt often found himself in the ironic position in the thirties of portraying a villain while at the same time doubling for the star (usually John Wayne). This sometimes led to the ridiculous situation in the last reel of Canutt chasing himself!

He was at his most active at Republic, organizing a whole team of accomplished stuntmen and properly trained horses and raising the hazardous rough-and-tumble craft of stunting to an efficient fine art.

Harry Carey Jnr (b. 1921) has never attained the status of his famous father, mainly because his youthful looks have caused him to be stereotyped in 'likeable kid' parts. But he has become a substantial and familiar support in many major

Westerns since his 1946 début in *Rolling Home*, most notably those directed by John Ford, who has given him the protégé treatment since his father's death in 1947. Junior was one of the *Three Godfathers* in Ford's film dedicated to the memory of Harry Carey Snr.

He has looked best when partnered with another Ford favourite, the more rugged Ben Johnson, a particularly happy teaming in *Wagonmaster*. His other impressive credits include most of Ford's Westerns since 1949 plus *Red River*, *Rio Bravo*, *The Comancheros*, *Shenandoah*, *Alvarez Kelly*, *Big Jake*, *One More Train to Rob* and *Something Big*.

Far left below: Harry Carey Jnr in *Wagonmaster* (1950) with Ruth Clifford and (behind) Joanne Dru. *Below left:* Rod Cameron in *Trigger Trail* (1944). *Right:* Rory Calhoun in Jacques Tourneur's *Way of a Gaucho* (1952). *Below:* Yakima Canutt in *'Neath Arizona Skies* (1934) with John Wayne.

Tall, thin, gaunt, eloquent, well-mannered **John Carradine** (b. 1906) has been a distinctive supporting actor in Westerns from the time DeMille heard him doing Shakespeare and cast him in *Sign of the Cross*. Usually the cunning villain, he achieved his best role as the posh gambler in *Stagecoach*, gallantly caring for delicate Louise Platt and perishing at the point of saving her with his last bullet from a fate worse than death at the hands of the Apaches.

He was also in *Drums Along the Mohawk*, *Western Union*, *Johnny Guitar*, *The True Story of Jesse James*, *Cheyenne Autumn*, and *The McMasters*. . . .

Western fans will remember Scottish-born **Andy Clyde** (1892–1967) as the actor who supplied the comedy relief as Windy (or Breezy) Holliday in the Hopalong Cassidy movies. Otherwise he spread himself wide in films, becoming adept at grizzled old men.

No list of screen heavies would be complete without the name of the greatest fall guy of them all, the ever-victimized **Elisha Cook Jnr** (b. 1906) – for years a Familiar Face but at last becoming recognized by his name as well.

Diminutive, pale-eyed, vulnerable Cook began his downtrodden career in 1936, but made no Westerns until the fifties. He made up for lost time in *Shane* by impulsively taking on Jack Palance who gunned him down in the first palpably realistic shooting on the Western screen. Since then he has invited scorn and humiliation in *Thunder Over the Plains*, Delmer Daves's *Drumbeat*, *The Indian Fighter*, *One-Eyed Jacks* and *Welcome to Hard Times*.

John Dehner (b. 1915), another Familiar Face,

played the shrewd, smooth, intelligent villain in numerous 'B' Westerns for the ten years after his film début in 1945. Then he was cast sympathetically as Sheriff Pat Garrett, father-figure to Paul Newman's Billy the Kid, in Arthur Penn's controversial *The Left-Handed Gun*, a serious, substantial part more suited to his ability. He also featured as the toughest and coolest of the Tobin gang who rough up Gary Cooper in *Man of the West*, and has since broadened his scope a good deal.

An accident in his youth gave **Andy Devine** (b. 1905) his chief asset in the movies: while a teenager he fell with a stick in his mouth and did irretrievable damage to his throat and vocal chords, a mishap which left him with the high-pitched, husky voice that became his familiar trademark as a tubby character comedian in scores of Westerns.

Devine (real name Jeremiah Schwartz) entered movies in 1926 as an extra but had little success until the coming of sound. Even then his obvious potential as comic relief was not spotted straight away, and in *Law and Order* (1932), for instance, he played a victim of rough justice, hanged for an accidental killing. Then his big, shy, soft-hearted, slow-witted country-boy characterization caught on, and he embarked on numerous second-feature Westerns, including a spell as sidekick to Roy Rogers in the forties. He also appeared with distinction in less modest films, notably as the stage-driver in *Stagecoach*, and also in two more Ford Westerns, *Two Rode Together* and *The Man Who Shot Liberty Valance*. In the fifties he became even better known in his TV role as 'Jingles', sidekick to Guy Madison's Wild Bill Hickok.

Even the most avid credits collector probably has difficulty in connecting the name **John Doucette** with the Familiar Face to which it belongs. But

no Western fan worthy of the name would fail to recognize him. He has specialized in light character parts, his stocky frame and pleasant, rugged features fitting him for the role of storekeeper or good farmer rather than villain. His films since *Station West* in 1948 include *Broken Arrow, Rancho Notorious, The Far Country, The Sons of Katie Elder, Nevada Smith, Big Jake* and *One More Train to Rob.*

Far left above: John Dehner despatched by Gary Cooper in *Man of the West* (1958). *Above left:* Andy Devine in *On the Old Spanish Trail* (1947) with Roy Rogers. *Above:* John Doucette restraining Steve McQueen in *Nevada Smith* (1966). *Right:* John Carradine. *Below:* Elisha Cook Jnr in *Shane* (1953) with Van Heflin and Jean Arthur.

Left: Dan Duryea in *Al Jennings of Oklahoma* (1951) with Gale Storm. *Below:* Frank Ferguson (with cup) in Fritz Lang's *Rancho Notorious* (1952) with Marlene Dietrich and Arthur Kennedy. *Right:* Jack Elam in *Once Upon a Time in the West* (1969). *Below right:* 'Wild' Bill Elliott (with characteristic reversed holsters) in *Tucson Raiders* (1944).

Though not exclusively a Westerner (*The Little Foxes* and *The Burglar* were among his finest films), **Dan Duryea** (1907–68) was at his toughest and most corrupt in his Westerns. With his thin voice, brushed-back hair, dangerously impudent face and surface charm he was perfect as the vicious, sneering, psychopathic villain in such Westerns as *Along Came Jones*, *Winchester '73* and (softened up a little) *Six Black Horses* – though he could be pleasant as in *Al Jennings of Oklahoma*.

In modern dress, with his sharp suits, fancy ties and the manner of an out-and-out cad, he remains firmly rooted in the forties – but in Western clothes he will prove far more durable.

The thought of **Jack Elam** (b. 1916) as a hotel manager or an accountant is faintly ludicrous when one recalls his many Western roles as a leering, treacherous gun-slinger. But he had both these jobs before entering films in 1950. Recently he has begun to feature high in the cast list as a comic heavy, character villain or crusty old-timer, but his years as a laconic, sinister, skulking thug were memorable – and made more so by his sight-

less left eye staring out sideways like a chameleon's. This eye is virtually the star of *Once Upon a Time in the West*, dominating the whole opening sequence as a doomed fly buzzes incessantly round it in close-up.

Among Elam's nastiest characterizations have been those in *The Man From Laramie*, in which he tries to knife James Stewart in the back, *The Comancheros*, in which he lays about Stuart Whitman with a rifle butt, and *The Pistolero of Red River*, in which he tries to blackmail Angie Dickinson. His send-up of a professional gunfighter was, more recently, the only redeeming feature of Burt Kennedy's terrible spoof Western, *Dirty Dingus Magee*, and he has begun to make it his speciality to save bad films, repeating the exercise in Hawks's *Rio Lobo*, in a simple-minded Disney production called *The Wild Country* and in Kennedy's *Hannie Caulder*.

'Wild' Bill Elliott (1903–65) was a struggling heavy for ten years under the name Gordon Elliott, initially in minor society parts and then in Westerns. His break came with a Columbia serial in 1938, *The Adventures of Wild Bill Hickok*, which gave him his change of name. Thereafter he made numerous 'B' Westerns for another twenty years, enjoying a brief reputation in the late forties and fifties as the first exponent of a new 'realism' in series Westerns, which was in fact a harking-back to the austerity of William S. Hart.

In such films as *Bitter Creek*, *Kansas Territory*, *The Longhorn*, *Waco* and *Fargo*, Elliott scorned the Boy Scout behaviour which had prevailed since Tom Mix, drank if he felt like it, beat up the villain while holding a gun on him if necessary, and was not averse to playing ruthless outlaws (though ripe for reformation, of course). Elliott's adult Westerns did not maintain their quality and he remains a minor star, but at his peak he did offer a refuge from the Autry/Rogers phase.

Elliott will also be remembered for wearing his six-guns in reversed-holster fashion, butts forward, which did not impair his speed on the draw.

Frank Ferguson (b. 1899) is a Familiar Face of thirty years' standing who looks like the mild college professor he once was. His image is the calm but worried, well-dressed, dignified town official – mayor, lawman, influential tradesman – sometimes corrupt but usually righteously honest. His numerous credits include *They Died with Their Boots On*, *Fort Apache*, *Bend of the River*, *Johnny Guitar* and *Man of the West*.

Another Familiar Face, of even longer experience, is **Paul Fix** (b. 1902), who has run the gamut of character parts since the early twenties and has lately taken to playing mature lawmen – as honest, usually, as his face. *Virginia City, Red River, Hondo, West of Montana, Shenandoah, El Dorado* and *Something Big* are a few of his many Westerns.

Jay C. Flippen (1899–1971) is yet another Familiar Face, a leading character actor in Westerns from 1950, who was often seen as a weatherbeaten sheriff, tough and virtuous rather than corrupt. Long experience in vaudeville and on the stage explains his late entry into movies, first in *Winchester '73*, and subsequently in many good Westerns such as *The Far Country, Run of the Arrow* and *Cat Ballou*.

Leo Gordon (b. 1922) has become a particularly Familiar Face in brutally villainous parts since 1953, his small, cruel eyes and cold face suggesting more than a hint of mental instability in the characters he plays. His Westerns have by and large been minor, but *Hondo* and *McLintock!* are among them.

George 'Gabby' Hayes (1885–1969) was many people's favourite sidekick: toothless, bearded and an inveterate tall-story teller, sometime comic relief to both William Boyd and Roy Rogers.

Hayes spent twenty-eight years on the stage before making his film début (apart from work as an extra) in an early talkie, *The Rainbow Man* (1929). At first he was clean-shaven and played mainly villains, often in John Wayne horse operas; then in the middle of the thirties he took on his more familiar image of bewhiskered old-timer. Occasionally he was cast in large-scale Westerns such as *The Plainsman*, but for most of his 200-odd films he was a stalwart of the series Western.

Tim Holt (1918–73), son of the silent and sound action star Jack Holt, was somewhat unlucky in that he gave very creditable performances in two highly acclaimed films, Orson Welles's *The Magnificent Ambersons* and John Huston's *The Treasure of the Sierra Madre*, and yet spent most of his career in minor Westerns (apart from small roles in *Stagecoach* and *My Darling Clementine*). As a Westerner, however, he had a following up to the middle fifties when the 'B' Western died.

Left: Leo Gordon disarmed by George Montgomery in *Black Patch* (1957). *Below left:* Paul Fix (left) and George 'Gabby' Hayes (second from right) in *Tall in the Saddle* (1944) with John Wayne and Raymond Hatton. *Above:* Tim Holt (left) in Lesley Selander's *Guns of Hate* (1948) with Richard Martin. *Below:* Jay C. Flippen gunned down by Ward Bond in *The Halliday Brand* (1957).

Skip Homeier (b. 1929), former child actor, has been the Western's chief exponent of juvenile delinquency, typecast as the petulant, gun-slinging youth trying to prove something after he portrayed the young punk who shot Gregory Peck in *The Gunfighter*. The characterization has come off best in his two Boetticher Westerns, *The Tall T* and *Comanche Station*.

Henry Hull (1890–1977) was a Familiar Face whose career as a character actor spanned more than fifty years. He excelled at grizzled, ferrety old-timers who were often sly, mean and stupid, and he upstaged many an experienced star in such Westerns as *Jesse James* and *Colorado Territory*.

Another character actor who stuck to the stage for many years before going into films was **Arthur Hunnicutt** (b. 1911) who made a few Charles Starrett 'B' Westerns in the early forties before winning promotion to mainly 'A' features.

Tall, lean, bearded and likeable, his speciality is the slow-speaking country character whose hick manner disguises considerable shrewdness and intelligence. In *The Tall T* he is rather sadly killed off early on by cold Henry Silva, but thereby becomes part of buddy Randolph Scott's revenge motivation. He has also been distinctive in *Broken Arrow*, *The Big Sky*, *The Lusty Men*, *Cat Ballou* and *El Dorado*.

John Ireland (b. 1914), Canadian-born actor who went from stage to films in 1945, is a classic heavy with his slight stoop, menacing walk, grumpy voice and brooding, mean face with deep-set eyes. He has usually played a hired gun of less than outstanding ability.

His career has varied between major Westerns and obscure independent ventures. Twice he has been on the losing side of the OK Corral skirmish, the first time as Billy Clanton in *My Darling Clementine* and the second as Johnny Ringo in *Gunfight at the OK Corral*, in which he is unpleasant to Jo van Fleet.

Ben Johnson (b. 1920), a real Westerner from Oklahoma, has been one of John Ford's most appealing protégés and a stalwart of many fine Westerns since his début in *Three Godfathers*. In his maturity he has started to get leading parts either as heroic gunman (e.g. in *The Wild Bunch*) or, more interestingly, lovable grouch with a nice line in dry aphorisms (e.g. in *Chisum*).

A rodeo champion of some distinction, Johnson got into films by acting as horse-wrangler on Howard Hughes's *The Outlaw*, became a stunt-man and double for John Wayne, and was picked by Ford for some of his best roles in *She Wore a Yellow Ribbon*, *Wagonmaster*, *Rio Grande* and *Cheyenne Autumn*. He has also been in *Shane*, *One-Eyed Jacks*, *Major Dundee* and *Something Big*, and has one of the most impressive records of any supporting Westerner.

Far left: Henry Hull. Above left: Skip Homeier in
The Gunfighter (1950) with Gregory Peck and Karl
Malden. Above: John Ireland in Red River (1948)
with Montgomery Clift. Right: Ben Johnson in
Wagonmaster (1950) with Joanne Dru. Below:
Arthur Hunnicutt in Distant Drums (1951) with
Gary Cooper.

In the 1960s **Victor Jory** (b. 1902 in Alaska) began to get big parts, and with them well-deserved recognition as an excellent screen actor, in such films as *The Fugitive Kind* and *The Miracle Worker*. But for a long while after his film début in 1932 he was the mainstay villain in countless minor Westerns, one of the nastiest opponents a star could expect to encounter with his saturnine features and ability to devise very sticky ends. In *Canadian Pacific* he has Randolph Scott blown up by several hundred-weight of dynamite, though the dose proves not to be fatal ('He was too close,' explains explosives expert J. Carrol Naish. 'If he'd been just six feet away . . .').

Since his promotion, Victor Jory has revisited the Western once or twice, as an Indian chief in John Ford's *Cheyenne Autumn* and in Budd Boetticher's *A Time for Dying*, but it is a previous generation of Western fans who will remember him best.

Brian Keith (b. 1921), son of actor Robert Keith, began with a Western, *Arrowhead*, in 1952, but has suffered in his career from a surfeit of roles for Walt Disney. Away from such bland security, however, he has built up a decent reputation as humane, serious, hard-bitten types, most notably in Sam Peckinpah's first film, *The Deadly Companions*. In this he was the tough, taciturn gunfighter who accidentally kills Maureen O'Hara's child and insists on making amends by helping her take the coffin through Indian-infested country back to the grave of her husband.

In *Nevada Smith* he was excellent as the man who adopts Steve McQueen, and he was the cavalry officer in *Run of the Arrow* who opts for negotiation with the Indians and gets an arrow for his troubles. One of the most attractive stalwarts, Keith made only two Westerns in the 1970s, the unmemorable *Something Big*, 1971, which starred Dean Martin, and the excellent *Eagle's Wing* in 1979.

Arthur Kennedy (b. 1914) can play sympathetic or bad guy roles with equal facility, but he has been preferred in Westerns as the more insidious kind of villain: friendly, smiling, charming and smooth-talking on the surface, weak and corrupt underneath. His speciality is the affable type who befriends the hero and then turns out to be planning something illegal to his own advantage on the side. He let James Stewart down in this way in *Bend of the River*, and Glenn Ford in *Day of the Evil Gun* where he starts off virtuously enough but discovers that killing is fun.

He has also, since his début at the beginning of the forties, been a hard-working heavy in *The Man from Laramie*, a good guy in *Rancho Notorious*, and an unlikely Doc Holliday in the comedy episode in *Cheyenne Autumn*. His main asset is that he can really act.

Actors with faces like that owned by **Jack Lambert** (b. 1922) tend not to last more than a reel or two and he has been no exception. It's a Familiar Face, however, thanks to appearances as gun-slinging thug in numerous Westerns – the mean, narrow eyes, sullen mouth and generally moronic mien making it hard to believe that Lambert originally embarked on an academic career before turning to movies in 1943. His better-known credits include *Vera Cruz*, *Run for Cover*, *How the West Was Won* and *Four for Texas*.

Opposite page: Brian Keith (left). *Above left:* Arthur Kennedy in *Red Mountain* (1952) with Lizabeth Scott. *Above:* Victor Jory in 1935. *Below:* Jack Lambert (left) in *Day of the Outlaw* (1959) with Frank de Kova.

One of Hollywood's finest and most forceful character actors since the mid-forties, **John McIntire** (b. 1907) can adjust his lean, pleasantly wry features to display integrity or roguishness with equal facility as the role demands. In *The Lawless Breed* (1952), a whitewash job on Wes Hardin, one of the West's more unsavoury outlaws, he showed just how versatile he could be by playing both the father and the uncle of Rock Hudson, the one cruel and puritanical, the other rough and sympathetic.

McIntire has proved himself particularly adept at well-dressed urban roles (though not out of place in the saddle as he demonstrated as Ward Bond's successor in TV's *Wagon Train*), occasion-ally as the baddie who runs the town behind a corrupt sheriff as in *The Far Country*, in which he opposed honest James Stewart. In *Stranger on Horseback* he defied Joel McCrea's judge and in *The Kentuckian* he tried to best his kinsman Burt Lancaster. He has featured prominently in many good Westerns, including *Winchester '73, Apache, Two Rode Together* and *Rooster Cogburn*.

Victor McLaglen (1886–1959) was for many years Hollywood's leading star-heavy, and he made few Westerns – but as three of them were among John Ford's most memorable, he earns an honourable mention here.

McLaglen, a big man with a big grin – a kind of

Wallace Beery with an open heart – became known by the title of his first American film, *The Beloved Brute* (1925). British-born, the eldest of eight brothers (five of whom also appeared in films), he had been a prizefighter, gold prospector, army officer and vaudeville performer before becoming first a leading player in British silent films and then a Hollywood star. The recurring figure in his career was John Ford, who gave him his best parts in the thirties, in *The Lost Patrol* and *The Informer*, the latter winning him a Best Actor Oscar, and who picked him to play the sentimental, hard-fighting, whisky-swigging sergeant in the three cavalry films, *Fort Apache*, *She Wore a Yellow Ribbon* and *Rio Grande*. He will be remembered for this trio of parts if for nothing else.

He was the father of Andrew V. McLaglen, prominent among the newer Western directors of the sixties.

Below left: John McIntire in Anthony Mann's *The Far Country* (1955) with James Stewart and (at left) Jay C. Flippen. *Below:* Victor McLaglen in *She Wore a Yellow Ribbon* (1949) with Mildred Natwick and Joanne Dru.

151

Emile Meyer (b. 1903) is not so much a Familiar Face as an Unforgettable Mug. His large frame, brutish, aggressive face and slow, nasal bark have led him occasionally into roles as troubleshooting authoritarians (mostly tough cops and prison governors), but more often he has featured as uncompromisingly brutal villains.

His best Western part was probably in *Shane*, where he added a flourishing beard and persuasive eloquence to his armoury as the cattle rancher trying to rid the land of humble farmers.

Although he made relatively few Westerns, the large dimensions of **Robert Middleton** (1911–77; christened Samuel G. Messer) and the scale of his nastiness from his début in 1954 soon made a sizeable impression. Oily villains were his speciality, leering, lecherous and smooth-talking if there are handsome women in the plot. He operated best in bloated capitalist roles, such as his evil saloon-owner in *The Proud Ones*, in which he tries to get the drop on Jeffrey Hunter with the aid of a hidden derringer and is shot in the back for his pains – thus demonstrating to Hunter, who has been castigating lawman Robert Ryan throughout the film for the very same thing, that shooting someone in the back is sometimes justified.

George Montgomery (b. 1916), formerly a boxer, began as a stuntman in the late thirties, and after making his featured début in *The Cisco Kid and the Lady* in 1939, became one of the more capable of the Western's minor stars of the forties and fifties. Noted for his good looks and restrained playing, he never graduated to major Westerns, but achieved a respectful following. He was at one time married to singer Dinah Shore.

The leading star of minor Westerns in recent years until his tragic death in an air crash in 1971, **Audie Murphy** (b. 1924 in Texas) entered movies on the strength of his record as the most decorated American soldier of the Second World War. He later re-enacted his own wartime exploits in *To Hell and Back*.

Murphy's slight build and eternally boyish looks typecast him as the quiet, innocent-looking youth who packed a fast, lethal six-gun when roused. His first Western role, in fact, was a creditable interpretation of Billy the Kid in *The Kid from Texas*, following which he stuck almost exclusively to the genre. Occasionally he rose above second features, notably in Huston's *The Red Badge of Courage*, the third version of *Destry Rides Again*, called simply *Destry*, and Boetticher's *A Time for Dying*.

Warren Oates (1932–82) had the good fortune during his comparatively short career (he made his début in 1959 in *Yellowstone Kelly*) to be used by two major directors, and he therefore became a familiar stalwart in a very short time. Like his colleagues Strother Martin and L.Q. Jones, he was

Far left above: Emile Meyer (second from left) in *Drums Across the River* (1954) with Audie Murphy, Walter Brennan and Jay Silverheels. *Above left:* George Montgomery in *Battle of Rogue River* (1954). *Above:* Warren Oates (second from left) in *The Wild Bunch* (1968) with Ben Johnson, William Holden and Ernest Borgnine. *Right:* Robert Middleton in *The Lonely Man* (1957).

soon favoured by Sam Peckinpah in particular, achieving a high billing as one of *The Wild Bunch* after previous appearances in *Ride the High Country* and *Major Dundee*.

Oates was at first typecast as petulant, sometimes psychopathic heavies, weak and short on intelligence but unpredictably violent. In *There Was a Crooked Man* these weaknesses are exploited by cunning Kirk Douglas to an extent where Oates, by comparison, becomes almost a sympathetic character – and, as usual, a dead one.

Oates was also kept very well employed by Burt Kennedy, notably in *West of Montana*, *The Rounders*, *Return of the Seven* (where he plays a straight tough-hero role – and survives) and *Welcome to Hard Times*. In addition he starred in the Monte Hellman curiosity, *The Shooting*, with Jack Nicholson, and alongside Peter Fonda in the latter's own *The Hired Hand* – and he had clearly outgrown the humble status of a heavy.

George O'Brien (b. 1900), briefly an assistant cameraman and stuntman for Tom Mix, became a major star right at the beginning of his career by being picked for the lead in John Ford's epic masterpiece *The Iron Horse* (1924). He followed this with another Ford film, *Three Bad Men*, and a starring part in F.W.Murnau's classic, *Sunrise*, but he failed to sustain these heady heights and settled down to a long stint in series Westerns.

As a sagebrush hero, however, he was popular and long-enduring, his riding ability and impressive physique (he was known for a while as 'The Chest') suiting him for rugged action parts and keeping him going through the thirties and into the forties. In common with other Ford protégés from the silent days, he has popped up from time to time in small parts in the old man's Westerns, including *Fort Apache*, *She Wore a Yellow Ribbon* and *Cheyenne Autumn*.

Slim Pickens (b. 1919), real name Louis Bert Lindley, is a throwback to the days of the sidekick, coming closest in style to Andy Devine with his authentic Southern accent, hoarse voice, and flabby physique. In fact, he took the Devine part driving the stage in the remake of *Stagecoach*.

After a series of minor Westerns in the fifties, however, mainly with very minor star Rex Allen,

Above: Slim Pickens (right) in *The Deserter* (1971) with Ricardo Montalban and Woody Strode. *Above right:* George O'Brien in *The Fighting Gringo* (1939). *Right:* Robert Preston (centre) celebrating with Brian Donlevy in *Union Pacific* (1939).

Pickens has shown his worth by graduating to bigger parts and better films, including *The Sheepman*, *One-Eyed Jacks*, *Major Dundee*, *Pat Garrett and Billy the Kid*, and *Blazing Saddles*.

Robert Preston (b. 1917) established himself as a strong second lead in his first two Westerns, *Union Pacific* (1939) and *Northwest Mounted Police* (1940) – and remained one until he achieved stardom on Broadway in the fifties.

Sporting a handsome moustache, Preston was usually called on to play cheerful, roguish characters, basically decent but with moral flaws in their make-up – the kind of heavy who dies contentedly in the hero's arms after redeeming himself with an act of bravery. Since he made his name on the stage, Preston has featured prominently in *How the West Was Won* but is no longer a regular Westerner.

Robert Ryan (1913–73) was, without any doubt, for thirty years one of Hollywood's finest and most intelligent actors, yet seriously under-estimated and starved of really substantial leading roles. It is ironic that in real life he was a genuine American liberal – while on the screen he earned his biggest reputation as a conveyor of intense hate, often racially motivated. Certainly no-one else could narrow an eye or curl a lip or make his voice tremble with such devastating effect.

As a Westerner, Ryan could play straight as well as crooked – his hunted killer in *The Naked Spur* and his ageing lawman (losing his vision at crucial moments) in *The Proud Ones* being equally memorable. In his later roles he became basically sympathetic – as the horse-handler in *The Professionals*, as William Holden's weary, reluctant pursuer in *The Wild Bunch*, as the pacifist sheriff in *Lawman* – the exception being *Hour of the Gun*, in which once again he was the outlaw on the run, this time with a relentless Wyatt Earp (James Garner) in pursuit.

Ryan perhaps achieved more as an actor in other genres, but the Western would have been the poorer without him.

No list of Western stalwarts should omit a mention of the genre's most familiar Indian, **Jay Silverheels** (b. 1920). A full-blooded Mohawk, tall and imposing, Silverheels has portrayed Indians, good and bad, on the screen since he began as an extra in 1938, eventually consolidating his popularity by playing Tonto to Clayton Moore's Lone Ranger on television. Veteran Indian actor, Chief Thundercloud, also achieved fame as Tonto in earlier days.

Silverheels was Geronimo in *Walk the Proud Land*, and his many other films include *Yellow Sky* and *Broken Arrow*.

Crafty-eyed and usually villainous, **Ray Teal** (1902–76) is a Familiar Face who was featured in countless Westerns as corrupt sheriff or sly, smoothly dressed front man for the villains. He began in a Gene Autry vehicle, *Western Jamboree*, and a random selection of credits could include

Left: Robert Ryan in *The Professionals* (1966).
Right: Jay Silverheels as a Navajo chief in the Gene Autry vehicle *The Cowboy and the Indians* (1949).

Above: Ray Teal (left) in *Band of Angels* (1958) with Yvonne De Carlo. *Left:* Lee Van Cleef (right) in *Gunfight at the OK Corral* (1957). *Below:* Chill Wills (left) in *Loaded Pistols* (1949) with Gene Autry and Jack Holt. *Above right:* Will Wright (with hat and cane) in *Dallas* (1950) with Jerome Cowan, Ruth Roman and Leif Erickson.

They Died with their Boots On, Ramrod, Winchester '73, Run for Cover, Saddle the Wind and *One-Eyed Jacks.*

Occasionally he was on the side of the good guys, as in Boetticher's *Decision at Sundown,* in which he is the rancher who helps Randolph Scott get even with villain John Carroll.

It is strange to see **Lee Van Cleef** (b. 1925), now that he has achieved fame and fortune in Italian Westerns, still standing as the end-credits roll. Throughout the fifties, this arch-villain with slit eyes, cadaverous face and cruel voice could be relied on to get himself shot at some stage in the proceedings, though he might on occasion, as in *Ride Lonesome,* leave it until the last reel.

He began in *High Noon* and turned up frequently thereafter as dispensable baddie in Westerns big and small, the former including *Man Without a Star, Gunfight at the OK Corral, The Tin Star* and *The Man Who Shot Liberty Valance.* His spaghetti credits include *For a Few Dollars More, The Good, the Bad and the Ugly, Death Rides a Horse* and *Sabata,* which contrives to turn him into a James Bond of the West by endowing him with invulnerability and a coatful of ingenious gadgets. Van Cleef's rise to dubious stardom must be accounted a great loss to the ranks of the classic heavies, in spite of increasingly flamboyant performances such as that in the title-role of *Captain Apache.*

Ex-lifeguard and stuntman **Robert J. Wilke** (b.

1913) made his first film, *San Francisco,* in 1936 and has been a reliable heavy ever since. A Familiar Face of mean, shifty appearance topping off an impressively big frame, Wilke swelled the ranks of the villains in many Tim Holt and Charles Starrett Westerns before being featured as one of the gunmen in *High Noon.* Subsequently he has become a little more prominent in such Westerns as *The Far Country, Wichita, Man of the West, The Magnificent Seven, A Gunfight* and *The Hallelujah Trail.*

Chill Wills (1903–78) was the singer with the extraordinary gravelly bass voice who, with his Avalon Boys, accompanied Laurel and Hardy's delightful dance in *Way Out West* (1937). He then grew into one of the Western's outstanding character actors – a true Texan, humorous, homespun, whimsical and shrewd; the old-timer who can tell the younger fellers a thing or two.

After a spell with George O'Brien, Wills went on to make numerous Westerns, a good proportion of them large-scale, such as *The Westerner, Western Union, Billy the Kid, Rio Grande, From Hell to Texas, The Alamo, The Deadly Companions, McLintock!* and *The Rounders.*

Will Wright (1891–1962) was a Familiar Face who, from the early forties until his death, played just about every kind of supporting role that a Western might require – barman, storekeeper, sheriff, banker, judge. . . . If any one Western character actor were to be singled out as typical of the breed, the final choice might well be Will Wright.

THE DIRECTORS

Most of the major American film directors have at some time in their careers tried their hand at a Western – which is hardly surprising since the building of the West is such a significant part of American history. For the most part they have re-created a romantic, idealized, mythological West, far removed (except in spirit) from the real frontier.

Historically, the West was peopled almost entirely by young first-generation foreign immigrants; vast areas of it were arid and uninhabitable; townships were shabby, enveloped in perpetual dust except when it rained and the dust turned to mud; killings were infrequent; six-guns were inaccurate; and the women were rough. A few film-makers have attempted to tell it how it was – but the majority have stuck to folklore and legend.

A score or so of directors, led by John Ford, have made the Western their special domain, or have done their best work in the genre or made a significant contribution to it. These are the ones whose careers are looked at briefly in this chapter.

Not included here are Edwin S. Porter, G.M. (Broncho Billy) Anderson, Griffith, Ince and Hart, whose important and influential pioneer work has been described in earlier chapters. Also excluded are such names as Lambert Hillyer and R.G. Springsteen, whose output was prolific but confined almost entirely to undistinguished 'B' pic-

Left: Arthur Penn (on ladder) directing Dustin Hoffman and Chief Dan George in *Little Big Man* (1970). *Above:* Martin Ritt shooting *Hud* (1963).

tures, although Hillyer did begin promisingly as a writer-director for Hart.

Others have left their mark on the genre but belong more properly to a film book of more general aims. George Stevens, as the director of *Shane*, cannot be ignored – but he made only one other Western, the insignificant and forgotten *Annie Oakley* (1935). *High Noon* is Fred Zinnemann's sole excursion West apart from the musical, *Oklahoma!* Robert Aldrich, best known for *The Big Knife, Whatever Happened to Baby Jane?* and *The Dirty Dozen*, made *Apache* and *Vera Cruz*. Fritz Lang, Austrian emigré who has specialized in many-layered thrillers, contributed *The Return of Frank James, Western Union* and *Rancho Notorious*. The late Wesley Ruggles, one of the original Keystone Cops, directed the classic *Cimarron* and the undistinguished *Arizona* but no other Westerns. Edward Dmytryk began his career with a Western in 1935, *The Hawk*, but has returned to the genre only rarely, with *Broken Lance, Warlock, Alvarez Kelly* and *Shalako*. The irrepressible Michael Curtiz, whose middle name was versatility, added a few Westerns, such as *Virginia City* and *The Comancheros*, to his huge output of entertainments. Nicholas Ray will be remembered for *The Lusty Men, Johnny Guitar, Run for Cover* and *The True Story of Jesse James*. Robert Parrish has received some acclaim for *The Wonderful Country* (but not for *A Town Called Bastard*). Samuel Fuller demands attention for *Run of the Arrow*. And Arthur Penn, when he has added more Westerns to his already considerable *Little Big*

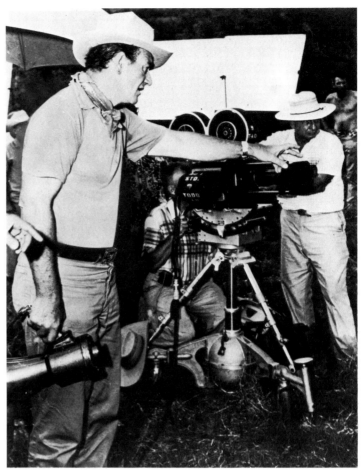

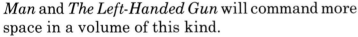

Man and *The Left-Handed Gun* will command more space in a volume of this kind.

'My name's **John Ford**. I make Westerns' is how America's greatest director of outdoor movies once described himself – and if that is how posterity remembers him, it will have made the right decision.

Ford (1895–1973) chose to be disparaging about his Westerns, calling them a mere relaxation from more exacting kinds of film work. But this can largely be put down to his celebrated irascibility, an impatience with probing interviewers, and a dislike of those critics and journalists who tried to turn him into a 'cult'. For he also said: 'I love to make Westerns. If I had my choice that's all I would make.'

Ford's monumental film career (almost 200 features in all) was by no means confined to Westerns. Indeed, as his career progressed all the recognition that was accorded to him was for his non-Westerns – it was films like *The Informer, The Grapes of Wrath, How Green Was My Valley* and *The Quiet Man* which won him his Oscars. It was only comparatively late in his career that he was acclaimed above all else for his Westerns; that he was recognized as the great poet and romanticist of the West.

Above, from the left: Four directors at work – Robert Aldrich on *Four for Texas* (1963) with Ursula Andress; Edward Dmytryk on *Broken Lance* (1954) with Spencer Tracy; John Huston on *The Misfits* (1961) with Eli Wallach; and John Wayne on *The Alamo* (1960). *Left:* On location for Fritz Lang's *Western Union* (1941). *Below:* Robert Mulligan directing *The Stalking Moon* (1968) with Gregory Peck and Frank Silvera.

An Irish-American, Ford was born Sean Aloysius O'Feeney (or O'Fearna if you're Irish) in 1895 of parents who had emigrated from Galway. He was the last of thirteen children. He visited Ireland several times as a boy.

Ford went to Hollywood in 1913 to join his elder brother Francis who was an actor-director at Universal. He started as a labourer, prop man and assistant director, and he was also a featured player, even contriving to appear in Griffith's *Birth of a Nation* as a member of the Ku Klux Klan. At this time he called himself Jack Ford and continued to do so until *Cameo Kirby* in 1923.

In 1917 he made his first film as a writer-director-actor, a two-reeler called *The Tornado* which he himself has described as 'just a bunch of stunts', and then directed *The Soul Herder*, the first of his twenty-six films with Harry Carey (who usually starred in the role of Cheyenne Harry) and the film he regards as having launched him as a director. It also marked Hoot Gibson's first appearance in a Ford film. In the same year Ford directed his first feature, *Straight Shooting*, which was also in the Cheyenne Harry series, and went on to make a large number of features and two-reelers with Carey, Gibson, Buck Jones and Tom Mix.

One of Ford's favourites among his early work was *Marked Men*, which derived from the 1916 *The Three Godfathers* and which was remade by William Wyler in 1929 as *Hell's Heroes*, by Richard Boleslawski in 1936 as *Three Godfathers* and by Ford again in 1948 as *Three Godfathers* (and as a tribute to Harry Carey). In 1920 he made *Just Pals* with Buck Jones, a film which displayed his growing understanding of simple people, his attention to background detail, his ability to draw natural performances from his actors, and his penchant for comedy.

The film which put Ford at the top of his tree was *The Iron Horse* in 1924. This epic about the building of the first transcontinental railroad was his first great success and it became a classic of the genre. His second great film of the period was the unsung *Three Bad Men* (1926), a delightful Western with a powerful landrush sequence and a number of Ford trademarks, including riders on the horizon and long-distance shots of wagons and men on the move.

Then followed the long period in Ford's career devoid of Westerns. He made many fine films in the thirties, including *Men Without Women*, *Arrowsmith*, *The Lost Patrol*, *The Informer*, *Steamboat Round the Bend* and *Wee Willie Winkie*, but it wasn't until 1939 that he returned with *Stagecoach*

to the genre at which he excelled. It was a triumphant return, however, *Stagecoach* proving, after Cruze's *The Covered Wagon*, the most influential Western in movie history.

Drums Along the Mohawk, Ford's first film in colour, came out the same year and then, after a few years' pause, he produced in half a decade (1946–50) his best and most satisfying Westerns: *My Darling Clementine*, *Fort Apache*, *She Wore a Yellow Ribbon*, *Wagonmaster* and *Rio Grande*. Six years later, with the mood of optimism tempered by hints of bitterness, melancholy and regret, came *The Searchers*, followed by *The Horse Soldiers*, *Sergeant Rutledge*, *Two Rode Together*, *The Man Who Shot Liberty Valance*, *How the West Was Won*

(Battle of Shiloh episode) and *Cheyenne Autumn*.

Ford's most distinctive work – and that includes many of his Westerns – dealt with the growth of America. He made films about most of the significant episodes in his country's history – the early colonization of the West, the Civil War, the extermination of the Indians, etc. – and in so doing he recounted the American saga in human terms and made it come alive. His epic canvases are peopled with ordinary men and women as well as with great historical figures, and above all he strove to show, with a blend of beauty, poetry and excitement, the relationship of those ordinary people with the land and with each other: men as pioneers and men as brothers.

John Ford and his films . . . *Far left and above left:* Ford directing *Stagecoach* (1939). *Above:* Ford on the set of *The Man Who Shot Liberty Valance* (1962) with James Stewart, Vera Miles and John Wayne. *Below left:* Irene Rich and Harry Carey in *Desperate Trails* (1921). *Below: Cheyenne Autumn* (1964) – and Monument Valley.

At the same time Ford also celebrated the Western way of life and mourned its passing – although depicting it how it should have been rather than how it was. His approach was emotional, not cool and detached like most Western directors; his vision of the West was very personal, the warmth and spontaneity of his films more than compensating for their occasional lapses into mawkishness and low comedy.

Ford's Westerns were nevertheless made with great efficiency and care. He said that he cut and shaped his films in the camera as he shot, leaving little for an editor to do ('There's not a lot of film left on the floor when I've finished'). He also declared himself a traditionalist in his methods, preferring black and white to colour, the old standard screen shape to wide-screen processes ('I like to see the people, and if you shoot them in wide-screen you're left with a lot of real-estate on either side'), and the use of a regular company of familiar actors, such as Ben Johnson and Ward Bond and many lesser lights.

In his finest films Ford was able to combine visual flair, exciting action, honest sentiment, genuine tenderness, subtle character detail and the ability to extract strong performances from limited actors (the supreme example being John Wayne) to a degree unmatched by any other director of Westerns. 'With Ford at his best,' Orson Welles said, 'you feel that the movie has lived and breathed in a real world.'

Budd Boetticher (b. 1916) has attained a considerable reputation as a director on the strength of a gangster thriller, a couple of films about bull-fighting and half a dozen medium-scale Westerns made to a commercial formula and built around a declining star. These few films have been highly acclaimed, and analysed and written about at great length – initially by serious French critics, later by American and British counterparts. Boetticher has, in fact, become a 'cult' figure.

The surprising thing is that, where the Westerns he made with Randolph Scott are concerned, the reputation is fully deserved. These modest, raw, tough, deceptively simple movies have an edge and a depth rarely achieved in other Westerns of comparable size and scope. And they have performed the rare double feat of pleasing serious cineastes *and* making money at the box-office. What is more, they have launched a number of names well known to Western fans, including Lee Marvin, Richard Boone, Henry Silva, Craig Stevens, Richard Rust, James Best, James Coburn and Claude Akins.

Boetticher, who had been a professional matador in Mexico, began in films as technical adviser on Rouben Mamoulian's bullfight picture, *Blood and Sand* (1941), and then worked his way up from assistant to fully fledged director, making his first Western of any significance, *The Cimarron Kid* with Audie Murphy and James Best, in 1951. In that year, too, he made *The Bullfighter and the Lady*, his first really successful film, which John Ford helped him to edit. More Westerns followed in 1952 and 1953 – *Bronco Buster, Horizons West*

Left: Budd Boetticher directing straight from the saddle; the film is *Comanche Station* (1960) with Randolph Scott. *Above left: Buchanan Rides Alone* (1958) with Peter Whitney, Craig Stevens and Scott. *Above right:* Scott in *Decision at Sundown* (1957). *Right:* Glenn Ford in *The Man from the Alamo* (1953).

with Robert Ryan, *Seminole* with Rock Hudson, *The Man from the Alamo* with Glenn Ford, and *Wings of the Hawk* with Van Heflin – and then in 1956 the fruitful association with Randolph Scott began with *Seven Men from Now*.

In the next four years this partnership produced (often with Burt Kennedy as scriptwriter) *The Tall T, Decision at Sundown, Buchanan Rides Alone, Ride Lonesome, Westbound* and *Comanche Station*, only one of which, *Westbound*, failed to make the grade in an original and highly individualistic group of Westerns. Subsequently, Boetticher exiled himself from Hollywood in order to concentrate on his strongly personal film about the great Mexican matador, *Arruza*, but returned to the Western in 1969 with *A Time for Dying*.

Boetticher's best Westerns are in fact powerfully influenced by his love of bullfighting, his heroes (always played by Randolph Scott) invariably appearing as proud lone combatants, like matadors, battling for survival in an arena (the West). The analogy can be extended by seeing the villains (always the most interesting of Boetticher's characters) as bulls, fighting blindly but even more

desperately for their own survival. The death of Lee Marvin in *Seven Men from Now*, felled by a single bullet from Scott before he has even had time to draw his gun, in particular is reminiscent of the slaying of a bull by the clean thrust of the matador's sword.

Like the director himself, Boetticher's characters are loners – alert, intelligent, completely at home outdoors in male company, but hard done by and disenchanted. In Boetticher's words they 'decide to do something because they want to do it. If they get killed on the way – and most of them do – it is because their desire can't be accomplished without a struggle.'

Among those who survive are the Scott heroes, men of integrity, intent on 'living the way a man should', but invariably obsessed by vengeance for the murder or abuse of a wife. They survive, but they are as much the losers as the dead villains, gaining little satisfaction and much despair from their mission of revenge.

Boetticher's style is marvellously simple and economical, sticking closely to the same plots, locations and character types in each of his

Westerns and stressing movement and action rather than ideas. Uncompromising violence (Richard Boone shot in the face in *The Tall T*; a wounded man, his foot caught in a stirrup, dragged along by his horse in *Comanche Station*) is offset by the humour of Kennedy's script and Scott's dry, ironic performances.

At his peak, Boetticher has produced some of the most satisfying Westerns ever made – and he has done so with a quarter of the budget and in a fraction of the time spent by other directors on more ambitious but far less successful projects.

In his heyday **James Cruze** was Hollywood's highest-salaried director, earning an unprecedented $7,000 a week in 1927. Yet he was not a great director and his reputation rests rather insecurely

Left: Randolph Scott and Noah Beery Jnr gaining the upper hand in Boetticher's *Decision at Sundown*. *Right:* James Cruze. *Below:* Shooting *The Covered Wagon* (1923) in Snake Valley, Nevada.

on a single film, *The Covered Wagon*, which was the first real epic Western and the first to involve large-scale location shooting.

Cruze was born in 1884, one of twenty-three children. He worked in a medicine show and later became a movie actor, achieving a brief reputation in a 1914 serial called *The Million Dollar Mystery*. He made his first film in 1918, and in 1923 embarked on the project that was to become one of the biggest commercial successes of its time and an immeasurable influence on the Western genre. *The Covered Wagon* captured the contemporary public's imagination with its size and splendour and superbly photographed Western vistas (though nowadays it appears slow and tedious and rather poorly acted). It gave the Western a popularity which has never waned and it guaranteed its director a permanent place in the history of the Western film.

Cruze made only three other Westerns in his seventy-film career – the disappointing follow-up to *The Covered Wagon*, *The Pony Express* (1925), and two sound films, both of which flopped badly, *Helldorado* (1934) and the epic *Sutter's Gold* (1936).

The latter film was a major disaster, in fact, and Cruze did little else of importance before he died in comparative poverty in 1942.

Delmer Daves (1904–77) is often named as the Western genre's most underrated director (perhaps because he never made a Western on an epic scale) and it is true that for a long time his originality was overlooked. He is the documentarian of the Western film, a director who, even more assiduously than William S. Hart, attempted to depict the West realistically as well as artistically.

This possibly stems from the fact that his own family had a pioneer background, his grandfather having made covered wagon crossings and been a Pony Express rider and he himself having spent some of his youth among Hopi and Navajo Indians. Daves began in films as a property assistant on Cruze's *The Covered Wagon* and made a career as a writer and actor until he directed his first film in 1943. His initial success came with the influential *Broken Arrow* in 1950, the first film since the days of Griffith and Ince to show the Indian as an intelligent human being ('Up to that time they were all

"Ugh! Ugh!" Indians'). A beautiful and humane film, it contained one of Daves's recurring themes – love and friendship based on mutual respect (in this case, the bond between Indian and white man, played by Jeff Chandler and James Stewart). Daves made another film about Indians, *Drumbeat* (1954), which he reckoned to be the most authentic of his movies.

The hallmark of Daves's Westerns is their authenticity. Where Ford pictured the West as it should have been, Daves tried to recapture the West as it was. There is no romanticism or sensationalism, and he sets his characters as part of a working community – in *Jubal* they are ranchers, in *Cowboy* they are cattle drovers, and in *The*

Right: Delmer Daves at work on a shooting script.
Below left and below: Two of Daves's Westerns, both with Glenn Ford – *Jubal* (1956) and *Cowboy* (1958).

Hanging Tree they are miners, and in each case there is a wealth of incidental background detail. And against these backgrounds, Daves tells his stories in a visually stunning but straightforward manner: 'I much prefer the audience not to know that there's a director. That's my general thesis in regard to directing.'

Cowboy is also a demonstration of Daves's insistence on always doing a dangerous stunt himself first if he expected an actor to do it, e.g. moving among the wild longhorn bulls for the scene where Glenn Ford has to ring the horn of one such bull. In the climactic cattle truck scene, Ford and Jack Lemmon – inspired no doubt by Daves's example – refused doubles when the script called for them to move among the closely packed, panicking steers.

Daves also made a pleasant contemporary Western, *Return of the Texan*, which is notable for a dominant performance by Walter Brennan, but his two great achievements after *Broken Arrow* are *3.10 to Yuma* and *The Last Wagon*. *3.10 to Yuma* is a classic among suspense Westerns, minutely observing the nature of heroism as ordinary guy Van Heflin single-handedly runs baddie Glenn

Ford in. *The Last Wagon*, a drama of survival in the desert as maligned Richard Widmark leads a wagon train to safety through Indian territory, is rugged and action-packed, one of the most exciting Westerns ever made.

Daves certainly proved himself one of Hollywood's most talented directors, at least in the Western genre, and in his later years he at last got the recognition he deserved.

Cecil B. DeMille (1881–1959) was a showman rather than a director, a man who made films 'as though chosen by God for this one task'. He will forever be associated with lavish biblical epics full of sex, violence and bathing scenes, but his eye for spectacle embraced the Western as well.

His first film, a Western called *The Squaw Man* (1913), was one of the first feature films shot in Hollywood and a subject he remade twice, in 1918 and 1931. He subsequently made a number of silent Westerns, including *The Virginian* (which shared the same star as *The Squaw Man*, Dustin Farnum) and *The Girl of the Golden West*.

Then in the late thirties and early forties he

made his epic Westerns, which are notable mainly for their extravagant budgets, corny, cliché-ridden dialogue and strong casts. *The Plainsman*, a highly romanticized account of the lives of Wild Bill Hickok, Calamity Jane and Buffalo Bill, gets by thanks to Gary Cooper's presence and the supporting acting of players like Fred Kohler and Porter Hall; *Union Pacific*, an account of the first railroad West highly derivative of *The Iron Horse*, is the strongest dramatically; and *Northwest Mounted Police* is an actionless bore in spite of Gary Cooper.

DeMille made one more Western, *Unconquered* (1947), also with Cooper.

André de Toth (b. 1900), a Hungarian director who was once a cowboy and who has worked in Hollywood since 1940, has carved a small niche in Westerns with his careful, composed style and technical proficiency. His characters lack warmth, however, and unlike Boetticher he has not got the best out of Randolph Scott, the actor he has used most, in such Westerns as *The Man in the Saddle* (retitled *The Outcast* in Britain), *Carson City*, *The Stranger Wore a Gun*, *Thunder Over the Plains*, *Riding Shotgun*, and *The Bounty Hunter*.

De Toth has also used Joel McCrea (in *Ramrod*) and Gary Cooper (in *Springfield Rifle*).

Henry Hathaway (1898–1982) was one of the great Hollywood directors, a long-serving and versatile artist whose Westerns were as variable in quality as his other films.

He began as an actor in films at the age of ten, was a prop boy in 1915, and an assistant director in 1926. In 1932 he made his début as a director with a series of Zane Grey adaptations, many of them starring Randolph Scott, the best of which was *To*

'Ready when you are, Mr DeMille!' . . . *Left: Northwest Mounted Police* (1939). *Above and below: Union Pacific* (1939) with director Cecil B. DeMille (in bed) and stars Joel McCrea and Barbara Stanwyck. *Below left:* DeMille's first remake of *The Squaw Man* (1918) with Elliott Dexter (left), Theodore Roberts (third from left), Edwin Stevens (centre) and (grinning) Monte Blue. *Bottom:* André de Toth (left) with Nigel Davenport.

the Last Man, a thoughtful tale about feuding families. In 1936 he made the first outdoor film in colour, The Trail of the Lonesome Pine, a beautifully photographed but static affair with Henry Fonda, and in the early forties he directed two moderately rated Westerns, Brigham Young, the story of the Mormons' trek West, with Dean Jagger and Tyrone Power, and The Shepherd of the Hills with Harry Carey.

Hathaway's best Westerns, however, all came in the latter part of his career, beginning with Rawhide (1951) with Tyrone Power, and continuing with From Hell to Texas, the highly enjoyable burlesque North to Alaska, most of How the West Was Won, The Sons of Katie Elder, Nevada Smith, Five Card Stud (which Hathaway didn't think much of) and True Grit.

Hathaway's strong points were atmosphere, character and authentic locations. He took particular care with locations, proud of being one of the few directors to handle their own second-unit work, and when this element combines successfully with the other two the result can be very impressive indeed. The little-known From Hell to Texas is quoted by those who have seen it as Hathaway's best Western on these three counts, a film directed with profound feeling for the deliberate pace and loneliness of the real West. Set in an authentically ramshackle township, its story of a sincerely religious cowboy (Don Murray) forced to become a killer is a perfect blend of action and mood.

Hathaway's other big achievement in the genre was True Grit, the Western which finally won John Wayne his long-service Oscar and saw him acting his age at last – a fat old man with an eyepatch; a drunk, a thief and a killer; but also a sympathetic, timeless image of the Old West.

'Today,' said Hathaway once, 'we tell it as it is, or was.'

Howard Hawks (1896–1977) was, like Budd Boetticher, a commercially successful Hollywood director who was then turned into a 'cult' figure by serious critics on both sides of the Atlantic. He filmed less than half a dozen major Westerns on top of his considerable output of thrillers, comedies and action dramas, yet he is the Western director most often put on a pedestal alongside John Ford.

Hawks himself never appeared over-impressed. Students of film insist on finding depths of complexity in his films' character inter-relationships and the thematic relationship of one film to another – yet he claimed that he was not a director of ideas, that his desire was only to tell a story, and that he made films purely as entertainment for mass audiences. 'I'm interested,' he said, 'in having people go and see the picture, and enjoy it.'

Of Westerns he said: 'To me a Western is gun-play and horses. . . . They're about adventurous life and sudden death. It's the most dramatic thing you can do.' Hawks did not in fact make a Western of any substance until *Red River* in 1948, thirty years after he began in films as a writer and editor. *Red River* is, however, a major Western epic and

Henry Hathaway (*left*) in the thirties — and three of his films: (*below left*) *Garden of Evil* (1954) with Gary Cooper and Richard Widmark; (*right*) *Rawhide* (1951) with Tyrone Power; and (*below*) *Five Card Stud* (1968) with Dean Martin.

virtues of energy, realism, harshness and a sense of scale.

After *Red River* Hawks made *The Big Sky*, which is the least of his Westerns, and chiefly notable for a finger amputation scene played for laughs by Kirk Douglas. Then came the second great Hawks Western, *Rio Bravo*, deservedly a classic and one of the most impeccably constructed Westerns ever produced.

Rio Bravo is the antithesis of *High Noon*, and the clearest exposition of Hawks's philosophy of professionalism. His sheriff (played by John Wayne) solves his own problem and doesn't go out looking for amateur help (though he welcomes volunteers and in fact depends on them); what is more, he wins by displaying superior skills and quicker wits. It is a traditional, straightforward film, good-humoured and exciting, but also rich in original touches.

Hawks's two Westerns after *Rio Bravo* – *El Dorado* and *Rio Lobo* – while enjoyable enough are merely imitations of the earlier film and not a patch on it, although there is some deliberate burlesque in *El Dorado*. His massive reputation as a director of Westerns virtually rests, then, on just two films – but these are sufficient to reveal a highly skilled, intuitive film-maker, and one who managed to satisfy large audiences and serious critics alike within a commercial system.

one of Hawks's best films. Set against a massive and realistic cattle-trade background, it exposes the violence beneath the difference in moral outlook between an older and a younger man (John Wayne and Montgomery Clift) which comes to a head on a hazardous cattle drive from Texas to Missouri in pioneer days. It has all the Hawks

Joseph Kane (b. 1897), who began as an editor, became a resident director for Republic from the mid-thirties and made a prodigious number of competent but unambitious Westerns. He directed many of Gene Autry's early films, some with John Wayne such as *The Lawless Nineties*, *King of the Pecos* and *The Lonely Trail*, a number of the 'Three Mesquiteers' series, and over forty with Roy Rogers. Finally, he was put on to Republic's bigger productions, which included *The Plainsman and the Lady*, *Wyoming*, *Oh! Susanna*, *The Vanishing American*, *Duel at Apache Wells* and *Spoilers of the Forest*.

Burt Kennedy (b. 1923) is one of the more interesting, lively and active of Western directors of recent years, a former radio and TV writer who made his name in films by scripting the best of Budd Boetticher's Westerns.

He professes to have been strongly influenced by John Ford, and shows it by his attention to detail and his romanticism, by editing his films 'in the camera', and by favouring the use of regular, familiar actors from Western to Western. He sums up his own aims thus: 'I like to tell a small story against a big background.'

Kennedy is something of a hit-and-miss director, stronger on character and atmosphere than plot and ideas and far more at home when he allows his

Above left: Howard Hawks. *Below left:* Hawks with John Wayne on the set of *Rio Lobo* (1970). *Above:* Burt Kennedy's *The Deserter* (1971) with Woody Strode and Bekim Fehmiu. *Below:* Kennedy (centre) with Yul Brynner and producer Ted Richmond during the shooting of *Return of the Seven* (1966).

the hardest feat of all: an entirely successful spoof Western, *Support Your Local Sheriff*. This starred James Garner as the lawman who finds the West too tame and is thinking of emigrating to Australia where the real pioneers are, and it is an accurate as well as very funny send-up of Western conventions and clichés. Just how difficult it is to make an acceptable satirical Western was demonstrated by Kennedy's next attempt, *Dirty Dingus Magee*, a disastrously unfunny affair with Frank Sinatra and George Kennedy.

At the time of writing, Kennedy has a sequel to *Sheriff* in the pipeline, *Support Your Local Gunfighter*, also with James Garner, an improvement, one hopes, on the implausible *Hannie Caulder*, which has Raquel Welch as a gun-slinging bounty hunter, and confirmation perhaps that Kennedy remains one of the genre's most entertaining directors.

Henry King (b. 1888 or 1892 – sources differ) is a veteran director of all kinds of movies, including *Tol'able David*, *The Song of Bernadette* and *Twelve O'Clock High*, but among whose outstanding work is one of the finest Westerns from any period, *The Gunfighter* (1950). This austere, anti-heroic film about a weary, ageing gunfighter (Gregory Peck) striving to achieve regeneration while having to fend off young delinquents out to make a reputation for themselves by killing him in a gun-duel, has the slow-moving inevitability of classical tragedy – which is not pitching the praise too high. It demonstrates, too, King's penchant for characterization and feeling for time and place, which he stressed above action and melodrama.

King became an actor at twenty-one and a film

irrepressible sense of humour to take over. Thus the routine and relatively straightforward *Return of the Seven*, *Young Billy Young* and *The Deserter* (a formula Western in *The Dirty Dozen/Professionals* vein) are unremarkable, while *West of Montana*, *The Rounders*, *The War Wagon* and *The Good Guys and the Bad Guys* are brought to life by Kennedy's injection of high spirits.

It is not surprising, therefore, that Kennedy is the one director of Westerns to have brought off

director a few years later when he started making shorts in 1916. His early, silent Westerns usually starred William Russell and included *When a Man Rides Alone, Where the West Begins* and *Six Feet Four*. Then in 1926 he gave Gary Cooper his first decent film role in *The Winning of Barbara Worth*, the story of the harnessing of the Colorado River.

King has made only three other Westerns: *Ramona*, the 1936 version of the famous Indian love story; *Jesse James* (1939), a smoothly made whitewash job on the celebrated outlaw; and *The Bravadoes* (1958), a neurotic, improbable and rather unpleasant revenge story, again with Gregory Peck. But his place in the history of the Western is assured by *The Gunfighter*.

Anthony Mann (1906–67) is yet another Hollywood director of modern times who has been idolized, analysed and given the 'cult' treatment – mainly for his string of remarkable Westerns in the fifties (although he began as a director in 1942) and for his later epics, *El Cid* and *The Fall of the Roman Empire*.

For Mann the Western was 'legend – and legend makes the very best cinema'. He also reckoned 'the simpler and more primitive the story the better' – and indeed his Westerns are basically simple enough: they are about violence. They are also tough, grim, cruel and generally black in mood; strong on location work, taut, realistic and technically highly accomplished. Their settings are suitably wild and the heroes are placed in them like 'Prometheuses chained to their rocks'.

Mann's first Westerns, *Devil's Doorway* and *The Furies*, were not especially successful, but when he began his partnership with star James Stewart in

Above left: Burt Kennedy, John Wayne and Kirk Douglas on location at Durango, Mexico, for *The War Wagon* (1967). *Below left:* Henry King. *Far left below:* Warner Baxter as Alessandro in Edwin Carewe's *Ramona* (1928) which King remade in 1936. *Above:* Anthony Mann. *Below:* Mann's *The Man from Laramie* (1955) with Arthur Kennedy and an incapacitated James Stewart.

Winchester '73 the breakthrough was achieved. They went on to make together *Bend of the River*, *The Naked Spur*, *The Far Country* and *The Man from Laramie*, Stewart's dedication and determination to do a job well suiting the character Mann wanted to put on the screen admirably. Stewart spent hours, for example, practising cocking and firing a Winchester rifle correctly for his role in *Winchester '73*.

Mann also made *The Last Frontier*, with Victor Mature as a semi-savage who wants to earn a cavalry uniform and be a soldier; *The Tin Star*, with Henry Fonda and Anthony Perkins; the brutal *Man of the West*, his best film, with Gary Cooper; and the studio-bound *Cimarron*, with Glenn Ford, which Mann himself called 'a disaster'.

In the Stewart films and *Man of the West*, Mann's heroes are thoughtful men forced into hysterical violence by their need to avenge a wrong or blot out the past. They are neurotic and cynical – which is hardly surprising given the amount of rough handling they have to endure: in *The Man from Laramie* Stewart is dragged through a fire and has his hand shot through; in *The Far Country* he is shot up and thrown into a river.

Mann's villains are among the most corrupt, unbalanced and memorable to be found in any Western before or since, with Alex Nicol in *The Man from Laramie*, Robert Ryan in *The Naked Spur*, Dan Duryea in *Winchester '73* and the depraved, grandiosely evil Doc Tobin of Lee J. Cobb in *Man of the West* taking the highest honours.

If one ever needed convincing that Westerns are a genre to be taken seriously, the work of Anthony Mann would be evidence enough.

George Marshall (1891–1975) entered films as an extra in 1912 and began his career as a director with a series of Harry Carey Westerns in 1917. A veteran with over 400 features to his credit, he worked in many genres, his output showing an extraordinary variation in quality, but had most success in his Westerns. Marshall made some good action Westerns including a number with Tom Mix and *When the Daltons Rode*. He also tried his hand at Western musicals such as *The Second Greatest Sex* and the awful *Red Garters* – but he was at his best when he could infuse humour into his work. Setting aside *Fancy Pants*, an out-

and-out comedy with Bob Hope, the finest examples of this are *Destry Rides Again* and *The Sheepman*, both of which have basically serious themes but which manage at the same time to be funny at the expense of Western conventions. The first will always be remembered for Marlene Dietrich's splendidly erotic saloon girl wowing the cowhands with her rendering of 'See What the Boys in the Back Room Will Have', while the second has an unforgettable scene in which sheepfarmer Glenn Ford picks a fight with town tough guy Mickey Shaughnessy.

On form, Marshall was an original contributor to the Western genre.

Andrew V. McLaglen (b. 1920), son of the actor Victor McLaglen, built up a reputation in the 1960s as one of the most promising of post-war directors of Westerns, but he never fulfilled that promise with a really major work.

He is an efficient director with a feeling for scale, sentiment and strong casts (e.g. *The Way West* which co-stars Kirk Douglas, Robert Mitchum and Richard Widmark), whose best achievement to date has been *Shenandoah*, the story of a pacifist

Above left: Charles Drake and (Sergeant) Jay C. Flippen in *Winchester '73* (1950), directed by Anthony Mann. *Above:* George Marshall discussing a scene in *Texas* (1941) with William Holden and Claire Trevor. *Below:* Glenn Ford, another star of *Texas*.

Southern family caught up in the Civil War, with a characteristic performance from James Stewart.

McLaglen's other films include *McLintock!* with John Wayne, *The Rare Breed* with Brian Keith, Maureen O'Hara and James Stewart, *The Undefeated* with John Wayne, *One More Train to Rob* with George Peppard, and *Something Big* with Dean Martin and Brian Keith.

Sam Peckinpah (b. 1926) is without a doubt the most impressive director to arrive on the Western scene for many years – and the most controversial. He has shown a deeply felt personal interest in the West (he was brought up in the modern West on land homesteaded by his grandfather) and an original approach based on a mixture of romanticism, heroism, violence, death and losing out. For, in Peckinpah's own words, 'the Western is a universal frame within which it is possible to comment on today'.

After a successful career in television, including

Above: Andrew V. McLaglen directing Doris Day in her first straight Western role, in *The Ballad of Josie* (1967). *Below:* McLaglen's *Shenandoah* (1965). *Right: The Way West*, directed by McLaglen in 1967. *Below right:* Sam Peckinpah guiding Robert Ryan's movements in *The Wild Bunch* (1968).

production of the series *The Westerner* with Brian Keith, Peckinpah made his first film, the relatively optimistic *The Deadly Companions*. Then came the film which made his name, *Ride the High Country*, a poignant celebration of the lost values of the Old West, with marvellous one-off comeback performances from veteran Westerners Randolph Scott and Joel McCrea.

Major Dundee, which followed, was hacked about prior to distribution and did badly. Peckinpah clashed with his producers, and being intractable, he moved into a four-year period of inactivity. His return to the screen was triumphant, however, his 1969 film, *The Wild Bunch*, proving a success on all levels. Described as a 'blood ballet', this massive, violent film is a compendium of Peckinpah's themes: the West as a battlefield; the search for a personal identity; the pain of growing old in a changing society; the demise of the West; and the paradoxically romantic degradation of death. 'My idea,' says Peckinpah, 'was that *The Wild Bunch* would have a cathartic effect. No, I don't like

Above: Sam Peckinpah and William Holden discuss *The Wild Bunch. Below: Major Dundee* (1965) with Charlton Heston and Senta Berger. *Right:* Yul Brynner in John Sturges's *The Magnificent Seven* (1960).

violence. In fact, when I look at the film itself, I find it unbearable.'

By contrast, *The Ballad of Cable Hogue* is warm, non-violent, romantic, even religious. But it is also cliché-ridden. Much better was *Junior Bonner*, 1972, a modern Western with Steve McQueen as an ageing rodeo star. Also interesting was *Pat Garrett and Billy the Kid*, 1973, with James Coburn and Kris Kristofferson in the leads and Bob Dylan in a minor role as the town undertaker.

'Sam Peckinpah,' says Stella Stevens (a star of *The Ballad of Cable Hogue*), 'is a man who expects excellence. If you can't give of your best, he doesn't want you around. I don't blame him.' As to his place in the art of the Western film, another of his actors, Robert Ryan, has put it well: 'All the Westerns have been made. The only difference is style and Peckinpah's style is extraordinary.'

Lesley Selander (b. 1900) is the kind of director who sooner or later gets 'taken up' by serious students of film and finds himself promoted from

Left: The Magnificent Seven. Below left: Eva Marie Saint and Gregory Peck in *The Stalking Moon.*

the ranks of the neglected to those of the lionized. A former cameraman, he has since 1936 been a prolific director of Westerns, cutting his teeth on Buck Jones vehicles, Hopalong Cassidy pictures, and many of Tim Holt's horse operas.

By achieving a high standard of action and production values on a tight budget he has steadily improved the quality of his product over the years, and some of his minor 'A' features have definite merits. *Stampede* (1949), for example, with Johnny Mack Brown and Rod Cameron, is distinguished for its serious treatment of killing; and *Shotgun* (1953), with Sterling Hayden as a callous, sweaty lawman on an arduous mission, is outstandingly photographed in colour, contains some 'sophisticated' violence, and presents the Apache as both a reasoning human being and a cruel warrior.

Lesley Selander will probably have his day.

Like Selander, **George Sherman** (b. 1908) is a prolific director who has graduated slowly from second features to medium-scale Westerns. He

Below: Ride the High Country (1962) with John Anderson, John Davis Chandler, L.Q.Jones and Warren Oates.

began in the 'Three Mesquiteers' series, some with John Wayne, made a few Gene Autry pictures, and then directed a batch of Don 'Red' Barry films for Republic. Since then he has maintained a steady output of good-looking action Westerns, routine but efficient, including latterly *Big Jake*.

John Sturges (b. 1911), who began directing in 1945, has become respected as a conventional but very competent and successful maker of major Westerns who takes the genre very seriously. 'Westerns,' he says, 'are one form that will remain unchanged. They represent something almost mystical to many, many people. Perhaps it has something to do with the myths of how our nation was built.'

For Sturges, the West is a man's world, and his cool, hard, detached style, emphasizing action, excitement and the rugged environment of the frontier, endorses the point. He believes there are three essentials to every Western: 1. Isolation – a man standing alone with no hope of help from outside (e.g. Spencer Tracy's predicament in *Bad Day at Black Rock* when the telegraph lines are cut). 2. The issues are resolved by violence in the form of gunplay (e.g. *Gunfight at the OK Corral*, *Hour of the Gun*). 3. A man, or group of men compulsively take law and justice, rightly or wrongly, into their

own hands (e.g. *The Magnificent Seven*). He follows this up by saying: 'A Western is a controlled, disciplined, formal kind of entertainment. There's good and bad; clearly defined issues; there's a chase; there's a gunfight.'

Sturges's simple philosophy is contained in many fine Westerns. His first success was *Escape from Fort Bravo* (1953) with William Holden, which he followed with *Bad Day at Black Rock*, a contemporary drama; *Backlash* with Richard Widmark; the unsatisfactory *Gunfight at the OK Corral*, redeemed by its superb shoot-out climax and Kirk Douglas's performance as Doc Holliday; *The Law and Jake Wade* with Widmark and Robert Taylor; *Last Train from Gun Hill*, a repeat of *3.10 to Yuma* with Kirk Douglas opposing Anthony Quinn; the marvellously entertaining *The Magnificent Seven*; *Sergeants Three*, a comic remake of *Gunga Din* (which Sturges had helped to edit); *The Hallelujah Trail* with Brian Keith and Burt Lancaster; and

Above left: George Sherman's *Calamity Jane and Sam Bass* (1949) with Marc Lawrence, Howard Duff, Lloyd Bridges and Charles Cane. *Left:* John Sturges. *Above: The Hallelujah Trail*, directed by Sturges in 1965. *Right:* Kirk Douglas and Earl Holliman in *Last Train from Gun Hill* (1959).

one of the best of all Wyatt Earp movies, *Hour of the Gun*, with James Garner, Jason Robards Jnr and Robert Ryan. Not a bad portfolio by any standards.

King Vidor (1896–1982) was a long-serving and much-respected Hollywood grandmaster who received an honorary Oscar in 1979. A veteran from 1915 who assisted both Griffith and Ince, his distinguished career contained few Westerns, but two of them at least – *Billy the Kid* and *Duel in the Sun* – hold an important place in the history of the genre. These two films in particular, together with *Northwest Passage*, show Vidor's romantic vision of backwoods America and his love of natural landscapes; they share, too, an earthy quality which is missing from his more routine action Westerns, *The Texas Rangers* and *Man Without a Star*.

Billy the Kid and *Duel in the Sun*, made sixteen years apart in 1930 and 1946 respectively, are nevertheless both highly original pieces of work. The first, an early experiment in 70 mm wide-screen, depicted Billy as a Robin Hood figure aiding oppressed citizens, but stressed authentic and austere images and settings. Its townships are shabby and its characters lifesize and realistic; even Billy is

not essentially a heroic figure. The second, by contrast, photographed in rich colour, is extravagantly and grandiosely passionate and romantic and its characters are much larger than life. More importantly, in *Duel in the Sun* sex is, for the first time in a Western, the principal motivation and not just an incidental subplot.

Vidor will probably be remembered more for his non-Westerns such as *The Big Parade*, *Hallelujah*, *The Champ* and *War and Peace*, but his contribution to the genre is not insignificant.

Like King Vidor, **Raoul Walsh** (b. 1892) has had a long and distinguished career, having gained his experience by assisting D.W.Griffith. He was also an actor until he lost an eye in 1929, and played John Wilkes Booth, Lincoln's assassin, in Griffith's *Birth of a Nation*. Griffith also gave him his first chance as a director, sending him to Mexico to make *Life of Villa*.

Walsh made a number of interesting Westerns up to the late forties (though showing a sad decline since), including one of the earliest successful sound Westerns, *In Old Arizona*, which demonstrated that there was more to talkies than mere talk, and John Wayne's first (and, for a while, last) large-scale starring vehicle, *The Big Trail*. His

Far left and centre left: The enduring King Vidor. Left: Raoul Walsh. Above: John Wayne and Tyrone Power Snr in Walsh's *The Big Trail* (1930). *Below:* *The Tall Men*, directed by Walsh in 1955.

other films include *The Dark Command*, also with John Wayne; the Errol Flynn characterization of General Custer, *They Died with Their Boots On*, which some critics regard as one of the great Westerns; *Pursued*; *Cheyenne*; *Silver River*; the moody *Colorado Territory*, with Joel McCrea and Virginia Mayo; *Along the Great Divide*; *Distant Drums*; *The Lawless Breed*; *Gun Fury*; *O'Rourke of the Royal Mounted*; *The Tall Men*; and the silly British spoof Western which matched Kenneth More with Jayne Mansfield, *The Sheriff of Fractured Jaw*.

The career of **William Wellman** (1896–1975) embraced most genres, with a special predilection for aviation (e.g. the magnificent Oscar-winning *Wings* of 1927), but in the words of Kevin Brownlow 'he suggests an authentic figure of the Old West; tall and lean with a tough, weatherbeaten

Above: William Wellman in 1941. *Above right:* Henry Fonda, Mary Beth Hughes and George Meeker in Wellman's *The Ox-Bow Incident* (1942). *Below:* William Wyler directing Carroll Baker in *The Big Country* (1958). *Right:* Walter Brennan, Paul Hurst, Chill Wills, Gary Cooper and John Qualen in Wyler's *The Westerner* (1939).

face and a voice exactly like John Wayne'. With such an appearance it is not surprising that he also made several fine Westerns, one in particular showing him to be an innovator and a great director: *The Ox-Bow Incident* (1942). This simple, sombre, devastating indictment of lynch law revived the serious non-action Western with a social message.

Wellman's first Westerns were silent films with Dustin Farnum and Buck Jones, and later he made *The Robin Hood of El Dorado* with Warner Baxter; *The Great Man's Lady*, with the familiar team of Joel McCrea and Barbara Stanwyck; a decent biography of *Buffalo Bill*, also with Joel McCrea; the underrated and thoughtful *Yellow Sky* with Gregory Peck; the ill-used Clark Gable vehicle, *Across the Wide Missouri*; and the rather ineffective *Westward the Women* with Robert Taylor.

Since an apprenticeship in the late twenties devoted almost exclusively to making short Westerns, **William Wyler** (b. 1902) has added very few titles to the genre. But these few are of more than passing interest, demonstrating this director's essential seriousness, careful craftsmanship, variable style from film to film, and his dictum that 'the story is always the central problem in any picture I have directed'.

Hell's Heroes was Wyler's first sound Western – his first all-talking picture, in fact – a version of *Three Godfathers*, the story so beloved of John Ford. *The Westerner* was Wyler's next Western, made ten years later in 1940 and containing a superb performance by Walter Brennan as Judge Roy Bean. The film is renowned for its climax in which Brennan goes to a theatre and sits in an empty auditorium expecting to see Lily Langtry; when the curtain goes up, however, instead of Miss Langtry, Brennan is confronted by hero and ex-friend Gary Cooper pointing a gun at him.

Wyler's only other Westerns are *Friendly Persuasion* (1956) and *The Big Country* (1958), both unfairly knocked by the critics but both popular and entertaining. They share a genuinely pacifist theme which is somewhat overstated in the earlier film but which comes across very effectively in the impressive *The Big Country*. Gregory Peck's anti-traditional hero, performing his feats of strength and endurance in private and determined to love his enemies, is a particularly felicitous creation, while the scale of the State of Texas has never been better conveyed. There are better Westerns, but it is difficult to think of many which have been more enjoyable.

193

The SPAGHETTI WESTERNS

There is nothing new about Continental Westerns. They were being made in Europe – including England – soon after the turn of the century. French film-makers in particular were enamoured of the genre, producing one-reelers with such titles as *The Hanging at Jefferson City* and *Hooligans of the West*, and emulating the Americans' initial respect for the Indian in anecdotes like *White Fawn's Devotion*. And in the twenties, Germany turned out a number of Westerns, mainly of the James Fenimore Cooper backwoods variety, such as *The Last of the Mohicans* which starred horror exponent Bela Lugosi as the Indian hero Uncas. Later on, in the thirties and forties, Germany went in for more conventional imitations, slow but filled with action, the best of which, such as *Sergeant Berry* (1938), were vehicles for immensely popular native star Hans Albers.

Over the years the American Western has inspired film-makers from countries all over the world – Japan, India, Mexico, Russia, Sweden, Brazil – and one should note in passing the efforts by Britain to adapt the genre to suitable Commonwealth locations such as Australia (*The Overlanders*, *Eureka Stockade*) and South Africa (*Diamond City*, *The Hellions*). Yet when one speaks nowadays of non-Hollywood Westerns one is inevitably referring to the phenomena of the past

Left: The Good, the Bad and the Ugly (1966). *Above:* Henry Fonda in *Once Upon a Time in the West* (1968).

twenty years which, begun in Germany but swiftly taken over and transformed into a boom industry by the Italians, have become known with affectionate scorn as 'Spaghetti Westerns'.

These black, violent, amoral, surrealistic, noisy, naive, pretentious, ridiculed, revered and astonishingly popular and lucrative pastiches of the hallowed American Western owe their existence to an alliance of two factors. One was the realization that American Westerns were beginning to command a growing world market while the domestic audience dwindled (*The Magnificent Seven*, itself an adaptation of a Japanese film, *The Seven Samurai*, quadrupled its box-office take when it was released outside America); the other was the discovery that, since Hollywood was already making a large number of its films, including Westerns, in European locations such as Spain and Yugoslavia, it would be just as easy for the country which consumed the product to manufacture it as well.

Germany, in the early sixties, was the first European country to produce these full-blooded imitations successfully, swallowing the Hollywood clichés whole; not long afterwards Italy joined in, adding large doses of the newly fashionable blatant sex and violence.

The first German efforts were adaptations of stories by a native author, Karl May, who had died in 1920 and had never been anywhere near the real West, but who was a passionate disciple of Zane Grey. His characters, Old Shatterhand, the noble Indian brave Winnetou, and Old Surehand

were re-created for the German screen with Yugoslav assistance, and portrayed by American, French and English stars such as Lex Barker, Pierre Brice, Anthony Steel and Stewart Granger. *The Treasure of Silver Lake, Winnetou the Warrior, The Last of the Renegades, Old Shatterhand, Among Vultures* – local audiences lapped them up and the *nouvelle vague* of new-look Westerns was under way.

These so-called 'Sauerkraut Westerns' stuck to traditional themes, mainly involving Redskins, and the first Italian imitations also played safe by featuring legendary figures such as Buffalo Bill (portrayed by Gordon Scott in *Buffalo Bill, Hero of the Far West*), Wyatt Earp (in the person of Guy Madison in *Duel at Rio Bravo*) and Calamity Jane and Wild Bill Hickok (Gloria Milland and Adrian

Left: Pierre Brice and Lex Barker as the Karl May characters, Winnetou and Shatterhand. *Below:* Brice and Rod Cameron (as Old Firehand) in *Thunder at the Border* (1966). *Right:* Clint Eastwood in *For a Few Dollars More* (1965). *Below right:* Stewart Granger as Old Surehand in *Flaming Frontier* (1965).

Hoven in Joaquin L. Romero Marchent's *Seven Hours of Gunfire*), though paying no more attention to historical accuracy than Hollywood has done.

But the emphasis in Italian Westerns soon drifted away from traditional atmosphere and they swiftly established a quasi-Western style of their own, consolidated in the most celebrated 'Spaghetti' of them all, Sergio Leone's trail-blazing *A Fistful of Dollars* (made in 1964). This adaptation of another of Kurosawa's Japanese *samurai* films, *Yojimbo*, displayed many of the 'Spaghetti Westerns'' most consistent elements, including the use of an American actor as hero (Clint Eastwood, popular as a star of the television series *Rawhide*) and English/American pseudonyms for those of the cast and crew apprehensive about the film's reception (Leone was 'Bob Robertson', respected Italian actor Gian Maria Volonté became 'John Welles' and composer Ennio Morricone was dubbed 'Dan Savio'). Even though the Continental Western has now become firmly established and can claim some vestiges of respectability, the vogue for pseudonyms has persisted: hence, at various times, Frank Kramer, Vance Lewis and Calvin Jackson Paget

for directors Gianfranco Parolini, Luigi Vanzi and Giorgio Ferroni, and Montgomery Wood, Evelyn Stewart, Bud Spencer and Anthony Steffen for players Giuliano Gemma, Ida Galli, Carlo Pedersoli and Antonio De Teffé to mention just a handful.

With few exceptions, the Italian Western has a Texas-Mexico border setting with sadistic Mexican bandits much in evidence (presumably to allow the predominantly Mediterranean cast to look more convincing). Desert is the prevailing geographical feature, and the Civil War or its aftermath is a recurrent background. The most common hero (or anti-hero) is the mysterious gunfighter (such as Clint Eastwood's cheroot-smoking Man With No Name) or bounty-hunter, invariably unshaven. Violence, rape and torture predominate during the frequent action spots; there is often a singularly Italian emphasis on gross eating habits; and the villains (especially if they are Mexican bandits) are much given to coarse laughter about nothing. Big close-ups, slowly moving heads and lengthy, meaningful stares are equally conventional, while the inevitable prolonged build-up to a climactic gunfight has sometimes been eked out to a ludi-

crous degree, especially by Leone in his three Clint Eastwood films, *A Fistful of Dollars*, *For A Few Dollars More* and *The Good, the Bad and the Ugly*, the last of which ended with a triangular confrontation between Eastwood, Eli Wallach and Lee Van Cleef. Latterly, mechanical gimmicks have started creeping in, Parolini's *Sabata*, for example, sporting a whole armoury of deadly gadgets such as William Berger's guitar which doubles as a rifle.

Part of the 'Spaghettis'' continuing success has been due to the willingness of top commercial directors to go on making them. Apart from Leone, who has lately added *Duck! You Sucker*, with Rod

Above left: Clint Eastwood disposing of the dead in *For a Few Dollars More* (1965). *Above and right:* *The Good, the Bad and the Ugly* (1966) with Lee Van Cleef, Eli Wallach and Clint Eastwood.

Steiger and James Coburn, to his impressive array, noteworthy exponents include Sergio Corbucci (*Minnesota Clay, Django, Ringo and His Golden Pistol, The Hellbinders, A Professional Gun, Navajo Joe, Companeros*); Joaquin L. Romero Marchent (*Gunfight at High Noon, Seven Hours of Gunfire, Seven from Texas*); the German director of the *Winnetou* series, Harald Reinl; Sergio Sollima (*The Big Gundown, Face to Face*); and Duccio Tessari (*A Pistol for Ringo, The Return of Ringo*), while interesting contributions have been made by Carlo Lizzani (alias Lee W. Beaver), with *Let Them Rest* and *The Hills Run Red*; Damiano Damiani, with *A Bullet for the General*; Mario Bava, with *Roy Colt and Winchester Jack*; Giulio Questi, with *Django Kill*; and Tonino Cervi, with *Today It's Me – Tomorrow You*. At the same time, just about every American Western star and heavy on the circuit has got in on the act at some time or other. Apart from regulars like Lex Barker, William Berger, Eastwood, Van Cleef and Guy Madison, Italian Westerns have employed the talents of Alex Nicol (*Ride and Kill*), Cameron Mitchell (*Minnesota Clay* and *Killer's Canyon*), Henry Silva and the late Dan Duryea

Above: Giuseppe Colizzi's *Revenge in El Paso* (1968). *Right:* Alex Cord in Franco Giraldi's *Dead or Alive* (1967). *Below and below right:* Sergio Leone's *Once Upon a Time in the West* (1968) with Henry Fonda and Charles Bronson.

(*The Hills Run Red*), Joseph Cotten (*The Tramplers*, *The Hellbinders* and *White Comanche*), Eli Wallach (*The Good, the Bad and the Ugly* and *Revenge in El Paso*), John Ireland (*Hate for Hate*), Alex Cord, Robert Ryan and Arthur Kennedy (*Dead or Alive*), John Phillip Law (*Death Rides a Horse*), Jeffrey Hunter (*Find a Place to Die*), Chuck Connors (*Kill Them All and Come Back Alone*), Jack Palance (*A Professional Gun*), Ernest Borgnine (*The Desperate Men*) . . . and so on.

Native stars who crop up with some regularity include Franco Nero, Tomas Milian, Giuliano Gemma, Nicoletta Machiavelli and Gian Maria Volonté, while the most consistent supporting players have been Fernando Sancho and Frank Wolff.

Perhaps the highpoint of the 'Spaghetti Western' has been the blockbuster *Once Upon a Time in the West*, which has inspired a number of serious critiques and has been described variously as the best, the most pretentious, the most boring, the most artistic and the phoniest of all the Italian wave. Certainly it is one of the longest and boasts the most impressive set of credits. It was directed by Sergio Leone, was part-scripted by Bernardo

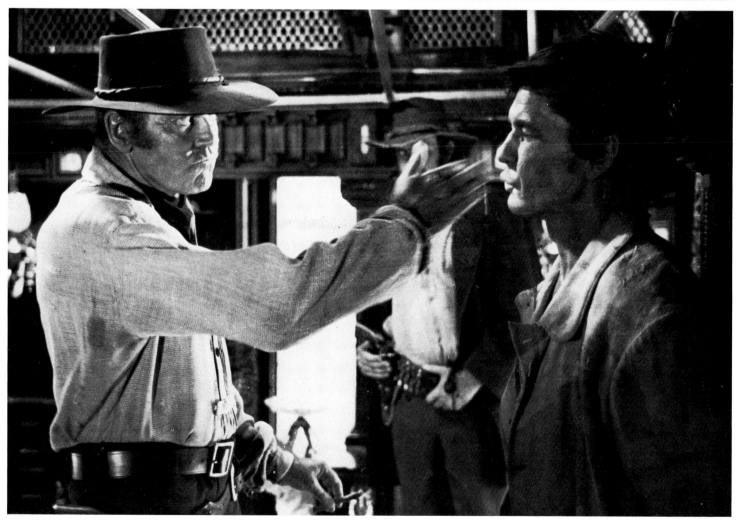

Bertolucci, has music by the genre's leading composer, Ennio Morricone (alias Dan Savio, alias Leo Nichols), and stars Henry Fonda, Claudia Cardinale, Jason Robards, Charles Bronson, Frank Wolff, Gabriele Ferzetti, Keenan Wynn, Lionel Stander, Jack Elam and Woody Strode.

One of the film's critiques typifies the kind of cult-inspired wild and woolly writing which has occasionally been perpetrated on behalf of the Italian Western. It makes the extraordinary statement: 'Of particular interest is the role of Henry Fonda as villain. He is at his worst when he is typecast. He shows, as for example in the bedroom scene with Claudia Cardinale, a complete misunderstanding of the spirit of the European Western.' If, as seems to be the implication here, Henry Fonda has really been typecast as a *villain* all these years, then his complete misunderstanding of the spirit of the European Western is hardly surprising.

This same critique reaches even headier heights (or lower depths, if you prefer) in a paragraph discussing the music scores composed for Italian Westerns, a much-discussed feature of the genre: 'In spaghetti music, a hysterical shriek may occur in a fight sequence, or may accompany a rider dashing off into the sagebrush. Overall, this seemingly arbitrary music establishes the picture's position in the universe.' Perhaps not all the hysterical shrieks are being confined to the screen. . . .

This kind of cult attention that has been paid to the European Western is, however, only a measure of its amazing success over less than a decade. So successful has the cycle been, in fact, that the Americans are now investing heavily in the Continental Western and most of the latest offerings are large-scale international co-productions which will receive world-wide distribution.

The final irony is that American Westerns are now showing a marked 'Spaghetti' influence, as revealed for example in the terseness and violence of films like *Hang 'Em High* (significantly, starring Clint Eastwood) and *Lawman*, in the bludgeoningly gory killings of *The Hunting Party*, and in the contrived and implausible plot of *A Gunfight*. The feeling one has is that the strands of myth and honest re-creation which connect the American Western to the real American West are being snipped away by those whose roots are far removed from the actual frontier – and one can only hope that the Kennedys, Peckinpahs, Boettichers and Hathaways will go on telling us how it really was . . . or at least how it might have been.

Below: Hang 'Em High – an American Western in 'Spaghetti' style. *Right and above right:* Howard Hawks's *Rio Lobo* (1970).

The TV WESTERNS

The volume of horse-opera output in something over twenty years of television transmission has been such that a complete survey of TV Westerns would require at least a whole book to itself. A brief chapter such as this, therefore, can do no more than outline the main developments, conventions and trends and illustrate them with the more popular and enduring series. Much of the output is, in any case, best ignored.

In the cinema in the early fifties the 'B' Western went into its final decline, and with it the last of the popular series stars such as Roy Rogers, Gene Autry, William Boyd, Charles Starrett, Tim Holt, Johnny Mack Brown, Bill Elliott, Wayne Morris, Rex Allen and Montie Hale. Many of them were ageing visibly and not being replaced, and only one or two, like Randolph Scott, survived and moved on to larger-scale Westerns.

The crunch factor was the rise in production costs. Quick, easy profits were no longer guaranteed, even less so as economy measures led to a product of increasingly poor quality. At the same time American television began to transmit batches of superior 'B' Westerns made from the thirties onwards, and not unnaturally, when the choice was between a 'cheap' new Western in the local picture-house and a good 'oldie' on the telly, audiences stayed at home.

Left: James Drury, star of the TV series *The Virginian*.
Above: Clayton Moore as *The Lone Ranger*.

With the demise of the 'Bs' and the whetting of the TV-viewing public's appetite with the showing of past cinema successes, the field was wide open for TV to start manufacturing its own Westerns tailored to the medium. This rebirth also gave some of the waning series stars a new lease of life.

Gene Autry, a shrewd businessman, had already anticipated the power of TV and had begun making several series aimed at children, one starring himself, others featuring Jack Mahoney (*The Range Rider*), Dick Jones (*Buffalo Bill Jnr*), Gail Davis (*Annie Oakley*), and his horse (*The Adventures of Champion – Champion the Wonder Horse* on British TV). All of these reached the BBC and Independent TV companies around the middle fifties.

Roy Rogers was not slow to follow Autry's example and took his wife, Dale Evans, and his horse 'Trigger' into a TV series – but he was less successful. William Boyd, on the other hand, was completely revived by TV, initially with a re-showing of all his old *Hopalong Cassidy* features, and then with an entirely new Cassidy series specifically designed for the small screen. His intentions were made quite clear when he said, *à propos* this new series: 'I have played down violence, tried to make Hoppy an admirable character and insisted on grammatical English.'

Legendary and historical characters were fully exploited as well as stars, including *Wild Bill Hickok* (with Guy Madison in the name part and Andy Devine as his sidekick, Jingles), *Kit Carson* (with Bill Williams), and more notably *The Cisco*

Kid and *The Lone Ranger*. *The Cisco Kid*, the O.Henry Western hero with the Robin Hood touch, was one of television's better efforts thanks to the utilization of the talents of such veteran large-screen directors as Lambert Hillyer; it had Duncan Renaldo playing the name part (well into his fifties, too) and Leo Carrillo providing the comic relief as Pancho. *The Lone Ranger*, although it suffered from a preponderance of very obvious studio sets, was no less successful – indeed, to heighten its mythical qualities, the programme's star, Clayton Moore, was contracted never to appear in public without his full regalia, including most importantly his black mask. The excellent Jay Silverheels played his Indian friend Tonto.

The power of the TV Western and its ability to make money were displayed at an early stage by the kind of exploitation in which titles and stars' names were lent to consumer products. But at the same time the limitations of putting the old formulas into the new medium were becoming apparent.

TV Westerns were (and still are) generally made with rigid requirements in mind, the important factor always being quantity rather than quality,

television's voracious appetite being what it is. At first the programmes were restricted to thirty minutes' running time – twenty-six minutes for the story, four for commercials (now, of course, they can run for an hour or, as with *The Virginian*, up to the length of a modest cinema feature); they had to provide an exactly timed dramatic highlight just before the commercial break; and to suit TV programming they had to prepare for a run of thirteen, twenty-six or thirty-nine episodes – many more than cinema series, which had never topped eight in one year. For speed, efficiency and economy, directors, cast and crew had to be maintained as a stock company.

Plots tended to be fast-paced, repetitive, vacuous, mild and restricted to action and simple comedy, often ending with all the main characters standing in a group having a good laugh (a convention by no means dead). The small screen also demanded a good deal of close-up work (unflattering to ageing stars like Autry and his contemporaries) and long static dialogue scenes. In addition, much of the action, 'exterior' as well as interior, was shot on studio sets with just an occasional stock chase scene filmed in the open as a sop to authenticity.

The largely bland and monotonous early TV Westerns declined in popularity just as the 'Bs' had done in the cinema, not least because the continued transmission of decently made old movies exposed their inferior quality. Thus in the early fifties a new kind of hard, gritty, 'adult' and 'realistic' TV Western was developed, strong on drama, psychology and characterization, with carefully understated acting, unusual stories, literate scripts and lots of moody atmosphere.

This fresh product was typified by *Gunsmoke* (re-titled *Gun Law* for its first transmissions in Britain), which was called 'the *High Noon* of broadcasting' and declared its abandonment of riding-shooting scenes, rescues of fair maidens from runaway stage-coaches and excessive gun-play. Into their place strode the tough, high-principled Marshal of Dodge City, Matt Dillon, 'upholding the law with the personal respect he commands'. This character made a huge box-office star of its portrayer, James Arness, a six-foot seven-inch discovery of John Wayne who had started as a singer, appeared in several Wayne Westerns, and played the title part of the 'vege-table' in *The Thing from Another World*. Like

Hugh O'Brian, though, who became equally famous in the title role of *Wyatt Earp* on TV, Arness never achieved equal stardom in his subsequent starring roles in the cinema.

No less familiar from *Gunsmoke* were the limp-ing, drawling deputy, Chester, played by Dennis Weaver, Milburn Stone's philosophical Doc and Amanda Blake's golden-hearted saloon-girl, Kitty.

The episodes increased their length from thirty minutes to an hour, and the series could boast Andrew V. McLaglen and Sam Peckinpah among its directors. It demonstrated, in short, the new and successful way to make horse operas for TV, and the formula became so popular that in 1959 no less than eight of America's top ten shows were Westerns, and several more virtual 'unknowns'

Far left above: Lorne Greene, ranch owner Ben Cartwright in *Bonanza*. *Above left:* James Arness, Marshal Matt Dillon in *Gunsmoke*. *Above:* Duncan Renaldo as the Cisco Kid in *The Gay Amigo* (1948), precursor of a popular TV series.

Above: Frank McGrath and Ward Bond in *Wagon Train. Below:* John Smith and Robert Fuller in *Laramie. Right:* Clint Walker as Cheyenne Bodie in *Cheyenne.*

found stardom in their own series – among them Clint Walker, Dale Robertson, Ty Hardin, Robert Horton – while a handful, including Clint Eastwood and James Garner, graduated successfully to the cinema screen.

Another popular series of the late fifties which endured long enough to expand from thirty minutes to an hour was the unpretentious *Wells Fargo*, which had the laconic Dale Robertson as its star, playing a special investigator for the famous Wells Fargo stage-coach company. One of the benefits enjoyed by this series was that its originator and writer of many episodes was Frank Gruber, who had been a novelist in the thirties and forties, had written for the legit screen (e.g. *The Kansan*, *Rawhide* and *Broken Lance*) and who later wrote scripts for *Wyatt Earp* and *The Texan*. Robertson later starred as the railroad boss in the *Iron Horse* series.

A less thoughtful series was *Cheyenne*, which chose to stress plot and action and the physique of its somewhat wooden star (Clint Walker, who stretched to just an inch less than James Arness at six feet six inches) rather than dialogue and deep philosophy.

Laramie was one of the first series to develop a necessary convention of TV Westerns – that of employing two stars, in this case John Smith and Robert Fuller. The filming of weekly hour-long series proved extremely rigorous and regular leading players found it less wearing to share top billing, with different stories tending to put the stress on one character or the other in alternate fashion. *Laramie*, set on a ranch and 'swing-station' in Wyoming, was a much-respected series which attracted many 'quality' guest stars, including Dan Duryea, Thomas Mitchell, Gary Merrill and Ernest Borgnine.

Another convention born of necessity was the Unsuccessful Romance. It was not possible to allow regular leading actors to indulge in lasting love affairs as this would mean introducing a new permanent character. Conversely, a star who tired of a series could conveniently be 'married off', as was the case with Pernell Roberts, one of the sons of ranch owner Ben Cartwright (played by Canadian actor Lorne Greene) in Paramount's phenomenally successful *Bonanza*. The other sons, the massive Dan Blocker ('Hoss') and Michael Landon ('Little Joe'), stayed the course.

This series, set on the so-called Ponderosa Ranch in the middle of Nevada silver-mining country, was so popular that in 1966, its veteran star, Lorne Greene, even topped the bill at the

London Palladium. *Bonanza* was another magnet, also, for established screen stars, such as Yvonne de Carlo, Ida Lupino, James Coburn, Robert Vaughn and, curiously, Ramon Novarro.

The only top contemporary cinema star to undertake a whole TV series of his own at this time was Henry Fonda in *The Deputy*. But the series was carefully titled, for Fonda, who played a marshal, had too many motion picture commitments to allow him to appear often, and the stories usually centred on the character of the dead-shot deputy portrayed by Allen Case. Veteran character actor Wallace Ford was also regularly involved. Another established star, Glenn Ford, has since appeared in his own series, the modernistic *Cade's County*.

The most rugged and atmospheric of the series at this time, and the one which purported to come closest to achieving documentary realism, was *Rawhide*, the creation of Hollywood writer Charles Marquis Warren, based on the great cattle drives of the 1870s. Eric Fleming played trail boss Gil Favor and Clint Eastwood found stardom as his ramrod, Rowdy Yates. R.G.Springsteen directed some of the episodes and Margaret O'Brien, Shelley Berman and Brian Donlevy were among the guest stars.

Another trend which began in the late fifties was the tongue-in-cheek Western series, typified by *Maverick* and *Have Gun, Will Travel*. Both these lighthearted affairs established their lead players as stars who subsequently climbed successfully on to the large screen – James Garner, as the wise-cracking gambler, Brett Maverick, and Richard Boone, as the travelling rifle expert, Paladin. When Garner became too big and too busy for *Maverick*, Jack Kelly successfully took over the starring role as brother Bart, and later Roger Moore joined the series as yet another sibling, Beau. *Have Gun, Will Travel*, given a good send-off in its first episode by the direction of Lewis Milestone, gained a reputation as a decently off-beat Western series and counted Andrew V. McLaglen among its regular directors and Sam Peckinpah among its writers.

Other series created new but less enduring stars, such as Ty Hardin in *Bronco*, the 'roving cowboy adventures' of Bronco Layne, and Will Hutchins in *Tenderfoot* (called *Sugarfoot* in the USA), an obvious crib of James Stewart's mild, peace-loving Destry. Attempts, too, were made to re-establish George Montgomery, in *Cimarron City*, and to mould the sullen young heavy of *Blackboard Jungle*, Jeff Morrow, into a more heroic

ideal in a railroad construction series, *Union Pacific*, but without noticeable success.

All but the hardiest Western series of the late fifties and early sixties, however, were overshadowed by the most celebrated TV horse opera of them all, *Wagon Train*. Inspired by John Ford's *Wagonmaster*, and given authenticity by the supervision of a Western historian and novelist, Dwight B. Newton, this series had a simple, very loose formula – a wagon trek from Missouri to the West Coast – which gave enormous scope for variety of plot and cast and mood. It had regular players – Ford veteran Ward Bond as wagonmaster Major Seth Adams (replaced by John McIntire after his death), and Robert Horton as tough scout Flint McCullough – but concentrated each week on the story of a different individual, played by a guest star. These ranged from Michael Rennie to Mickey Rooney, from Agnes Moorehead to Mercedes McCambridge, and in one purple episode no less a personage than Bette Davis betook herself to play the lead. Such was the programme's status, indeed, that in 1960 John Ford took time off to direct an episode, *The Colter Craven Story*, which was about General (and President) Ulysses Grant and featured John Wayne, under the pseudonym Michael Morris, as General Sherman.

On the strength of his new-found stardom,

Robert Horton later sustained a series of his own, *A Man Called Shenandoah*, but he has been little heard of since.

The above handful of major series were the best and most enduring of the TV Western's most popular period, but even as they settled comfortably into their weekly slots, over-exploitation was already eroding the genre's success. Series started after a while to create their own clichés and to strive too desperately for effect. Some, like *Jim Bowie*, with Scott Forbes as the knife-throwing frontiersman, were rather crude and unpleasant, while others were either imitative (e.g. *Steve Donovan, Western Marshal*, starring Douglas Kennedy, a copy of *Gunsmoke*) or gimmicky (like *Sky King*, the adventures of a flying Texas Ranger, or *Sheriff of Cochise*, with its modern setting) or too many stages removed from the real West (such as *Riverboat*, with Darren McGavin and Burt Reynolds, or *Frontier Circus*).

On the other hand, creditable attempts to disregard strait-jacketing continuity of character and storyline, such as *Frontier*, which devised a different plot and set of characters for each episode, were generally not successful – although *Zane Grey Theatre* did well for a while on the strength of its stories and stars, who included Jack Palance and excellent actors such as Dean Jagger and Ralph Meeker.

Unpretentious action aimed at youthful audiences was maintained in such series as the somewhat bland *Sergeant Preston of the Yukon* (which included Lesley Selander among its directors) and the surefire *Adventures of Rin Tin Tin*, while the Indians were decently taken care of by *Hawkeye and the Last of the Mohicans*, loosely adapted from James Fenimore Cooper, with Lon Chaney Jnr and John Hart, *Brave Eagle*, with Keith Larsen, and *Broken Arrow*, a very successful series based on the James Stewart/Jeff Chandler film, their roles as paleface and Apache respectively being adopted by John Lupton and Michael Ansara.

From the middle sixties to the present time, the popularity of TV Westerns has eased off to a less commanding level than hitherto, and series have tended to be fewer, more wordy, more carefully made, and relatively ambitious.

One of the longest-lasting has been *The Virginian*, based loosely on the Owen Wister character played previously on the cinema screen by Gary Cooper and Joel McCrea and portrayed in the TV version by James Drury (who has shared the lead with Lee J. Cobb, as Judge Garth, and Doug McClure, as Trampas). This hardy perennial, set in the town of Medicine Bow and on the Shiloh Ranch, has increased its length from an hour to feature dimensions, and has attracted such guest stars as (once again) Bette Davis, and Nancy Sinatra, Robert Redford and Neville Brand. It is a series with an ominously permanent look about it.

Another series which has endured is *The High Chaparral*, with Leif Erickson and Cameron Mitchell, about a family seeking roots in the newly won West – but one wonders whether it really merits the repeats it has been given by the BBC.

An interesting departure from convention is contained in *The Big Valley*, which has the matriarchal figure of Barbara Stanwyck as its leading character, the strong, self-reliant head of a pioneering family. This is, in fact, the culmination of the job done by TV in restoring women as important figures in Westerns – most likely in acknowledgment of the fact that women, as domestic consumers, are vital members of the viewing audience. Certainly female guest stars feature as regularly and as prominently as male.

The TV Western no longer rockets relatively unknown actors to stardom as it used to, though attempts have been made with Chuck Connors in *The Rifleman* (another series involving Sam Peckinpah as writer and director) and *Branded*, Wayne Maunder in *Custer*, and Michael Anderson Jnr in *The Monroes* (which has, however, spawned a promising cinema actress, Barbara Hershey). Rather have series of recent years relied on more established names such as the late Jeffrey Hunter (*Temple Houston*), Stuart Whitman (*Cimarron Strip*) and Neville Brand (*Laredo*).

Perhaps the latest trend on TV is indicated by the tongue-in-cheek series, *Alias Smith and Jones*, with the late Pete Duel and Ben Murphy, which bears a transparent resemblance to *Butch Cassidy and the Sundance Kid* in its quipping dialogue and the interplay of its outlaw heroes.

But whatever the trends, one must emphasize that the TV Western has only ever followed behind its big brother in the cinema. Television has only belittled the Western, it has never expanded its scope; it has never contributed to the genre in any way, nor could it ever emulate the scale and grandeur of the major motion picture Westerns. Saddest of all, perhaps, is TV's failure to exploit its documentary potential where the West is concerned. Apart from one or two isolated efforts such as *The Real West*, narrated by Gary Cooper, and a BBC 'Chronicle' programme, *The Fastest Con in the West*, TV has hardly bothered to try to convey frontier life authentically. And *that* is something TV could do well.

Above left: Doug McClure, Jeanette Nolan, James Drury, Sara Lane and John McIntire (replacing Lee J. Cobb) in *The Virginian*. *Above right:* Ben Murphy (right) and the late Pete Duel in *Alias Smith and Jones*. Right: Mark Slade, 'Billy Blue' in *The High Chaparral*.

INDEX

Figures in **bold** type indicate illustrations
Television films have (TV) after their titles

ACKNOWLEDGMENTS

The authors wish to thank the following for their valuable help: The Information Department and Stills Collection of the National Film Archive; Rosemary Stark; Paul Madden; Kenneth Thompson; and Mary Unwin.
Acknowledgment is also made to the following books and publications:
A Pictorial History of the Western Film by William K. Everson. Citadel Press, 1969.
The Western by William K. Everson and George N. Fenin. Ryan Press Inc., 1962.
Horizons West by Jim Kitses. Thames and Hudson, 1969.
Budd Boetticher: The Western by Jim Kitses. British Film Institute, 1969.
The Hall of Fame of Western Film Stars by Ernest N. Corneau. Christopher Publishing House, 1969.
John Ford by Peter Bogdanovich. Studio Vista, 1967.

Howard Hawks by Robin Wood. Secker and Warburg, 1968.
The Heavies by Ian and Elisabeth Cameron. Studio Vista, 1967.
The Western – An Illustrated Guide by Allen Eyles. A.Zwemmer/A.S.Barnes, 1967.

The publishers are grateful to the following for permission to reproduce film stills:
pp 208 top, 210, 211 top MCA (England) TV Ltd.
pp 208 bottom, 211 bottom NBC International, and to Mr Allan Hutchinson of C.I.C., Columbia Pictures, Metro Goldwyn Mayer, MCA-Universal, Mr Leslie Pound and Miss Pat Sukling of Paramount Pictures, London, Mr John Fairburn and Miss Barbara De Lord of 20th Century-Fox, London, Mrs Carol Futtrel of Warner Bros., London, and Mr M. Tither of United Artists, London.